POETRY IN AUSTRALIA
Volume II
Modern Australian Verse

Poetry in Australia

VOLUME II

MODERN AUSTRALIAN VERSE

chosen by

DOUGLAS STEWART

UNIVERSITY OF CALIFORNIA PRESS

Berkeley and Los Angeles

1965

University of California Press
Berkeley and Los Angeles
California

ACKNOWLEDGMENTS

ACKNOWLEDGMENTS for poems in this anthology are due to the following periodicals and publishers:

The *Atlantic Monthly* for "Eagles Over the Lambing Paddock" by Ernest G. Moll.

Australian Letters for "Hillside" by Alexander Craig, "Three Kings Came" by Thomas Shapcott, "Dust", "Ruins of the City of Hay" and "Strange Fruit" by Randolph Stow, "Bert Schultz" by Colin Thiele.

The *Bulletin* for "Breaking" by J. Alex Allan, "Chez-Nous" by A. G. Austin, "Cow Dance" by Bruce Beaver, "Spring Offensive, 1941" by Maurice Biggs, "Coronation Day at Melrose" by Peter Bladen, "Becalmed" and "Death of a Whale" by John Blight, "Harry Pearce", "Men in Green", "Night Sowing", "Ariel" and "Pallid Cuckoo" by David Campbell, "Independence" by Nancy Cato, "Daydreamers" by Norma L. Davis, "Methuselah", "The Raising of the Dead" and "Detail From an Annunciation by Crivelli" by Rosemary Dobson, "Variations on a Medieval Theme" by Geoffrey Dutton, "The Farm Near Norman's Lane" by Mary Finnin, "Back From the Paved Way", "The Face of the Waters", "The Wind at Your Door" and "Macquarie Place" by Robert D. FitzGerald, "Poems From the Coalfields" by Ian Healy, "Christmas 1942" by Eric Irvin, "Chanticleer" by Margaret Irvin, "Revelation" and "Bread" by Nancy Keesing, "Halfheard" by Christopher Koch, "Native Born" by Eve Langley, "Kangaroo by Nightfall" by Noel Macainsh, "Late Winter", "Canticle" and "New Guinea" by James McAuley, "The

White Eagle" by Nan McDonald, "Heat", "A Fairy Tale", "Table-birds", "An Old Inmate", and "Legerdemain" by Kenneth Mackenzie, "Recitative", "Au Tombeau de Mon Père" and "L'Après Midi d'une Fille aux Cheveux de Lin" by Ronald McCuaig, " 'Morning, Morning", "At a Time" and "Love and Marriage" by Ray Mathew, "Athlete" by Don Maynard, "Comrade in Arms" by T. Inglis Moore, "They'll Tell You About Me" and "Wilderness Theme" by Ian Mudie, "Back Lane" by R. D. Murphy, "Lalique" and "Sheep" by Hal Porter, "Wakeful in the Township" by Elizabeth Riddell, "Waratah", "The Lyre-bird", "The Tank" and "Rock-lily" by Roland Robinson, "Sheaf-tosser" and "Little Sticks" by Eric Rolls, "The Town" and "Mullabinda" by David Rowbotham, "Canberra in April" by J. R. Rowland, "The Finches" by Thomas W. Shapcott, "Night Out" by R. A. Simpson, "Bedlam Hills" and "The Last Summer" by Vivian Smith, "The Snow-gum", "Mahony's Mountain", "Brinda-bella", "Nesting Time" and "The Garden of Ships" by Douglas Stewart, "Fishing Season" by Val Vallis, "Love Poem" by Chris Wallace-Crabbe, "Idyll", "A Papuan Shepherd", "The Room" and "The Sea" by Francis Webb, "Rolling John" by A. J. Wood, "Wonga Vine", "Bullocky", "South of My Days" and "Storm" by Judith Wright.

Encounter for "Pietà" by James McAuley.

Meanjin for "The Sea and the Tiger" by Laurence Collinson, "Across the Strait" by Rosemary Dobson, "Prizegiving" by Gwen Harwood, "The Death of the Bird" and "Pyramis" by A. D. Hope, "Gordon Childe" by David Martin, "The Utopia of Lord Mayor Howard" by Randolph Stow, "The Hawthorn Hedge" and "Woman to Man" by Judith Wright.

Melbourne University Magazine for "Various Wakings" by Vincent Buckley, "In March" by Philip Martin.

ACKNOWLEDGMENTS

Outposts (London) for "Eyewitness" by Rodney Hall.

Poetry (South Australia) for "Burke and Wills" by Ken Barratt.

Prospect for "Late Tutorial" by Vincent Buckley, "Ancient Historian" by Chris Wallace-Crabbe.

Quadrant for "The Hatters" by Nan McDonald, "The Silkworms" by Douglas Stewart.

Southerly for "Generations" by Robert Clark, "Beach Burial" by Kenneth Slessor, "The Bull" by Judith Wright.

Sydney Morning Herald for "Noah's Song" by Evan Jones.

Angus and Robertson Ltd for poems from *Sunday at Yarralumla* by Ethel Anderson, *Poems of War and Peace* by Maurice Biggs, *A Beachcomber's Diary* by John Blight, *Masters in Israel* by Vincent Buckley, *The Miracle of Mullion Hill* by David Campbell, *The Living Sky* by Alexander Craig, *Earth Cry* by Norma L. Davis, *The Ship of Ice* and *Child with a Cockatoo* by Rosemary Dobson, *Poems* by Wolfe Fairbridge, *The Shield of Place* by Mary Finnin, *Southmost Twelve* by Robert D. FitzGerald, *Poems of Discovery* by William Hart-Smith, *Poems* by Gwen Harwood, *The Earthbound* by Charles Higham, *Circus at World's End* by Peter Hopegood, *A Soldier's Miscellany* by Eric Irvin, *A Vision of Ceremony* by James McAuley, *Pacific Sea* and *The Lighthouse* by Nan McDonald, *Collected Poems* by J. A. R. McKellar, *Selected Poems* by Kenneth Mackenzie, *The Ballad of Bloodthirsty Bessie* by Ronald McCuaig, *South of the Equator* by Ray Mathew, *Poems 1940-1955* by Ernest G. Moll, *Bayonet and Grass* by T. Inglis Moore, *The Blue Crane* by

Ian Mudie, *The Hexagon* by Hal Porter, *Forbears* by Elizabeth Riddell, *Inland* by David Rowbotham, *Poems* by Kenneth Slessor, *Sun Orchids, The Birdsville Track* and *Rutherford* by Douglas Stewart, *Phoenix Wings* by Harold Stewart, *Songs of the East Coast* by Val Vallis, *Beyond the Claw* by Brian Vrepont, *The Music of Division* by Chris Wallace-Crabbe, *A Drum for Ben Boyd, Leichhardt in Theatre* and *Socrates* by Francis Webb, *Woman to Man* and *The Two Fires* by Judith Wright.

Chatto and Windus Ltd for poems from *Speak with the Sun* by David Campbell.

F. W. Cheshire Pty Ltd for poems from *The Dogman* by Robert Clark, *No Fixed Address* by Bruce Dawe, *Flowers and Fury* by Geoffrey Dutton, *Four Poets* by Judith Green, Rodney Hall, David Malouf and Don Maynard, *Inside the Whale* by Evan Jones.

The John Day Co. Inc. (New York) and Dennis Dobson Ltd (London) for poems from *Selected Verse* by John Manifold. (Copyright 1946 by The John Day Co. Inc.)

E. J. Dwyer Ltd for the poem from *Speak to Strangers* by R. D. Murphy.

Edwards and Shaw Ltd for poems from *Apocalypse in Springtime* by Lex Banning, *The Two Suns Met* by John Blight, *Poems* by David Campbell, *Antipodes in Shoes* by Geoffrey Dutton, *The Wandering Islands* by A. D. Hope, *Deep Well* by Roland Robinson, *The Walk Along the Beach* by R. A. Simpson, *The Other Meaning* by Vivian Smith, *Thirty Poems* by John Thompson.

Georgian House Pty Ltd for poems from *Selected Poems* by Rex Ingamells.

ACKNOWLEDGMENTS

Hamish Hamilton Ltd for poems from *Poems* by A. D. Hope.

Jacaranda Press Pty Ltd for poems from *Time on Fire* by Thomas W. Shapcott.

Lyrebird Writers for poems from *The Darkened Window* by Nancy Cato and *Imminent Summer* by Nancy Keesing.

Lothian Publishing Co. Ltd for the poem from *Poems* by Furnley Maurice.

Macdonald Ltd for poems from *Outrider* by Randolph Stow.

Meanjin Press for poems from *With a Hawk's Quill* by James Picot, *The Moving Image* by Judith Wright.

Melbourne University Press for poems from *Squatter's Luck* by Ethel Anderson, *Moonlight Acre* and *This Night's Orbit* by Robert D. FitzGerald, *Under Aldebaran* by James Mc-Auley.

Overland Press for the poem from *The Moods of Love* by Laurence Collinson.

Rigby's Ltd for poems from *The North-bound Rider* by Ian Mudie, *Man in a Landscape* by Colin Thiele.

Robertson and Mullens for the poem from *Pools of the Cinnabar Range* by Flexmore Hudson.

Scorpion Press (London) for the poem from *Once Bitten Twice Bitten* by Peter Porter.

CONTENTS

CONTENTS

CONTENTS

CONTENTS

CONTENTS

CONTENTS

CONTENTS

B

CONTENTS

xviii

CONTENTS

INTRODUCTION

It so happened that when I was first thinking about this anthology, wondering on what principle the poems should be selected, how to find a clear track through all the poetry that has been written in Australia in the last thirty years, I picked up an English anthology which contained Wordsworth's "The Solitary Reaper"; and suddenly I remembered how enjoyable an experience the reading of poetry can be.

It is a simple fact which should never be forgotten; and surely it is the principle on which those who are free to read poetry for its own sake, without any other considerations, do their reading and choose their favourites. But when you are in the business of writing or criticizing poetry, surrounded and bombarded by controversy, you do tend to forget that this is an art meant to provoke not argument but pleasure.

People are always telling us how poetry should be written and what it ought to be about: that it should be about pylons, the compulsory subject-matter of the English poets of the thirties; that it should be (how far away that seems now!) about the Spanish civil war; that it should be about the workers; that it should be about religion; that it should be intellectual or that it should be simple; that it should always or never be in correct form; that, in Australia, it should always or never be about Australia.

All these conflicting opinions are, of course, right; for the Muse, thank Heaven, as a poet lately remarked to me when we were discussing a poem on road accidents, is various. Poets should write about what they want to write about. But in the midst of the uproar, which is chiefly instigated by book reviewers because their trade is to criticize and by new poets because they have to make a place for their poetry, how

few are the critics who pause to remind us, simply, that poetry
is enjoyable. "The Solitary Reaper" has itself been attacked
in this age by no less a poet than Robert Graves; who, in a
talk to a girls' school in America in 1957 which he reprinted
in *Steps* (1958), affected to take the poem literally and so
(partly by mis-reading the fourth line) found a few logical
inconsistencies in it. I suppose you could do that, too, to the
"Ode to a Nightingale" and the "Ancient Mariner"; and to
Shaw Neilson's "The Orange Tree", one of the most beauti-
ful poems ever written in Australia. But this sort of niggling
is a futile occupation.

And in fact through all the controversies, from year to year
and century to century, repeated in anthology after anthology,
the poems which people really enjoy go on living unper-
turbed:

> Behold her, single in the field,
> Yon solitary Highland Lass!
> Reaping and singing by herself;
> Stop here, or gently pass!
> Alone she cuts and binds the grain,
> And sings a melancholy strain;
> O listen! for the Vale profound
> Is overflowing with the sound.

Behold her, indeed!

Poetry can be "enjoyed", of course, in many moods and
many styles. The "terrible sonnets" of Hopkins are not less
pleasurable, in an exceedingly grim kind of way, than "Glory
be to God for dappled things". One does not expect from
the dramatic monologues of Browning or the rhyming essays
of Pope the same qualities as from the lyric. Whatever is
good in its kind is worth having and worth preserving. Yet
it seems to me that at all times, and particularly when choos-
ing the poems for an anthology, one should not lose sight
of the true and original meaning of "enjoyment". It means

giving joy; and in the long run, I feel often enough, that is what poetry is all about.

What, then, are the qualities which make "The Solitary Reaper" so supremely enjoyable a poem? It is a poem about the frailness of the Highland girl against the harshness of the Scottish landscape and the harshness of her peasant life; ultimately it is about the loneliness and the pathos and the courage of the human spirit. Against the darkness, she sings. But you can have equally beautiful poems on quite different themes. The key to its magic is in that word "overflowing". Its essentials are fullness of melody and fullness of emotion. It fills the universe while we are reading it; and the world is changed, if not (to quote the master again) to "an unsubstantial faery place" on this occasion, to this one pure melody.

Of course all poems do not stand on so high a peak as this. There are different levels, and different kinds, of genuine enjoyment.

As well as the more exalted virtues in poetry—melody and feeling in the lyric, structure and movement in the narrative—I like things that are alive, odd, humorous, out of the way. I like the touch of fantasy, light and graceful as in Rosemary Dobson's "Methuselah" or macabre as in John Blight's "Becalmed" and the poems of Eric Rolls. As well as the depth of thought and feeling I like the queerness of Ethel Anderson's "Kunai-mai-pa Mo" or the collection of lost souls in Nan McDonald's "Hatters". I enjoy Kenneth Mackenzie's "Pat Young" because it is so full of liveliness both of style and feeling, and Bruce Beaver's "Cow Dance" for its high spirits. I like the alert, contemporary note in Nancy Keesing's "Revelation" and Sylvia Lawson's "Trader's Return". I find my interest immediately captured by a surprising phrase or turn of thought, as when Max Dunn begins a poem with the statement "I danced before I had two feet", or Ray Mathew discovers that morning has a yellow crest like a cockatoo, or T. Inglis Moore demands to know who "the celestial C.O." is, or Vivian Smith in "The Last Summer" fills a whole poem with strange and haunting images. I like the tough Australian humour of Max Harris's "The Tantanoola Tiger", Francis Webb's "Idyll" and John Manifold's "The Bunyip and the Whistling Kettle"; the imagination in Bruce Dawe's picture of the dreaming dolls walking the city streets at midnight or Peter Hopegood finding a Passion play in the death of a moth; and the wit of John Thompson's "Letter to a Friend" and, in a very different vein, Hal Porter's investigation of the behaviour of sheep. I like the living portrayal of character, whether dramatic as in David Rowbotham's "Mullabinda", humorous and appreciative as in the countrymen of Colin Thiele, satirical as in Gwen Harwood's "Panther and Peacock" or profoundly human and humane as in Ronald McCuaig's "Au Tombeau de Mon Père". The thing I do not enjoy is dullness.

That is the outlook, then, from which the poems have been selected. Though I have not excluded any good poems merely because they are familiar, the resulting contents are more different from those of other anthologies than I had expected them to be; but that, though it is doubtless due partly to the principle on which the selection was made, is chiefly because of the period set down for it: from 1930 onwards. Since Brennan, Shaw Neilson, Hugh McCrae, Mary Gilmore and many others who wrote in the earlier years of this century were, after consultation with the calendar and discussion with Professor Inglis Moore, regarded as actually or essentially out of my period, I could not include these poets; but at the same time I was free to range wider among contemporary writers than most other anthologists have been able to, and also to give full weight to those—such as Slessor, FitzGerald, A. D. Hope and Judith Wright—who are outstanding among them.

I don't know that the result would have been very different had I chosen the poems on some alternative principle that might be considered more respectable. I suppose one could select simply the "best" poems for the period; but then, in my view, the best *are* the most enjoyable, or the most enjoyable are the best. I suppose one could choose each poet's most "important" poem; but then his most truly important poem would be, not necessarily his largest or most pretentious, but his most enjoyable.

There would naturally be a temptation, in assembling what is intended to be a representative Australian anthology, to choose poems about Australia; but that, when so many poets are naturally concerned with Australian themes, happens inevitably of its own accord, and it would be absurd to exclude good poems that did not happen to confine themselves to these territorial limits. One could choose, again, poems which "reflect the age". But then all poems necessarily reflect some aspect of the age they are written in, even if they are a criticism of or a retreat from it; and, however welcome they are when they occur, it would again be absurd, as it would be impossible, to restrict an anthology to poems which specifically set out to paint the contemporary scene. Robert D. Fitz-Gerald's "The Wind at Your Door", probing into the origins of Australian civilization, and William Hart-Smith's "Christopher Columbus", analysing that spirit of exploration which is now taking man into space, are not less "contemporary" than J. R. Rowland's amusing and highly up-to-date description of "Canberra in April".

And lastly, of course, an anthology of this kind should attempt to give as wide a picture as possible, consistent with quality, of Australian poetry in the period. That I have certainly tried to do; but without losing sight of the principle that it should be enjoyable.

Holding to this principle did not, as I say, make a great deal of difference to the final result. But it made a useful test for my artistic conscience, and a useful guide for decisions; and of course it must have to some extent affected the selection. It would account for what may seem some vagaries of choice, and it would account for the general drift, tone or direction of it.

It would explain, for instance, why, though I have included one vivid extract from "Five Visions of Captain Cook", I preferred to present Kenneth Slessor at some length in the less frequently anthologized "The Atlas". "Captain Cook" is a very fine poem, and we are perfectly entitled to place a special value upon it because the theme is Australian; nevertheless I think there are more variety, more subtlety, more of Slessor's particular qualities of sensuous imagination, humour and melody, in the sequence I have chosen.

It would explain, too, why among the poems of Judith Wright who, like Slessor, offers a most bewildering variety of possible choices to the anthologist, I have included "Wonga Vine". It is not one of her more "important" poems; it has no obvious intellectual content; it is not particularly Australian in the way that "Bullocky" is; yet, ever since I first read it many years ago, it has haunted me. It seems to mean so much more than it says, and it is so profound a piece of melody:

> Lie on my eyes like hands,
> let no sun shine—
> O twilight bell,
> flower of the wonga vine.

And it would certainly explain why—though they would probably have been included on any other sensible principle of selection—the anthology contains, as well as its odd, humorous and out-of-the-way pieces, such supremely beautiful poems as Slessor's "Beach Burial", Judith Wright's "The Old Prison", Eve Langley's "Native Born", David Campbell's "Night Sowing", Rosemary Dobson's "Detail from an Annunciation by Crivelli", A. D. Hope's "An Epistle", and Francis Webb's "Five Days Old".

The year set down for this volume to open—1930—was in a sense arbitrary, as are all attempts to divide the continuous, living stream of poetry into neat periods of time. Poetry does not alter so much over the years and over the centuries as we may be led to imagine.

Artificial styles may be developed, as in the eighteenth century or, earlier, in Spenser. Different kinds of subject-matter may become fashionable. Eccentricities of style may be developed, from inner necessity, by exceptional individuals such as Swinburne, Hopkins, Eliot and Dylan Thomas; and may be imitated, at their peril, by their followers. The language of even the most traditional kind of poetry must change as the language of the nation changes, or it will no longer be in touch with life. Yet through all the changes and all the deviations from the norm, right through English poetry from Chaucer to Browning, from Skelton to Auden, from Shakespeare to Yeats, runs a clear line of direct speech; what Hazlitt called in prose the "plain English" style. When Yeats laid down for modern times his most sensible rule that poets should use "the natural words in their natural order" he was only rediscovering the practice of Chaucer in *The Canterbury Tales* and the revolution of Wordsworth and Coleridge against the artifices of the eighteenth century. And when we read the verse of poets who practised this direct, natural speech we are impressed not so much by the difference between the speech of past times and our own, as by the similarity.

> . . . . Men must endure
> Their going hence, even as their coming hither.
> Ripeness is all.

Who could speak more directly than that?

In Australia as in England "modern" poetry cannot be separated from the poetry that went before it. Harpur, when he escaped from his Victorian and Wordsworthian conven-

tions in "A Midsummer Noon in the Australian Forest";
Bernard O'Dowd in much of his best poem, "The Bush";
Brennan in "The Wanderer" and in many of his shorter
pieces—wrote the kind of direct speech which most contem-
porary writers would employ; as also, besides familiarizing
us all with the Australian idiom and environment, did Pater-
son and Lawson in their bush ballads and on the rare occa-
sions when they stepped beyond their easy conventions to
write poetry of higher quality—Lawson in "Ballad of the
Drover", Paterson in "A Dedication":

> But all our ways are new and strange
> And through our blood there runs
> The vagabonding love of change
> That drove us westward of the range
> And westward of the sun.

Shaw Neilson, who is timeless; Hugh McCrae, whose best
lyrics are always clear and direct in spite of the antique cos-
tume he often chose to wear; Mary Gilmore, who continued
to write pithily until the day of her death in 1962—these
three writers were all represented in the annual anthology
Australian Poetry which started in 1941, and they could take
their place without question in an anthology of "modern"
Australian writing. So with others. It would have been quite
possible, no doubt, to begin a modern anthology in 1917 when
Leon Gellert's *Songs of a Campaign* was published.

But if the essential nature and style of poetry do not alter
very much from generation to generation, some changes do
nevertheless occur. In Australia the bush ballad, which had
been called into existence to celebrate horsemanship and the
droving days, gradually petered out as the twentieth century
replaced the horse with the car and the bullock with train
and truck. Language, imagery and subject-matter in more
serious poetry became, in general, more Australian and more
closely in touch with contemporary life. A poetry such as
Brennan's, in so far as it was studded with archaisms and

reflected the moods of Baudelaire and the nineties, would no longer be written, or written in the same way. The lighter notes of the nineties, as in the wine and roses of Victor Daley, catching something of their flavour from Ernest Dowson, would similarly go out of fashion. It would no longer be thought possible to write a poetry like Bernard O'Dowd's which, loaded with learned allusions, must have been intended, however unconsciously, largely for the information and instruction of an unlettered generation. The attitudes and the phenomena of the Celtic Twilight, as they were reflected in the poems of Roderic Quinn and David McKee Wright—both of whom had nevertheless considerable justification for writing about Ireland—vanished into the mists from which they came. The satyrs of Hugh McCrae, though they would be replaced later in the century by a re-examination of the Greek myths from a more scholarly and Freudian point of view, would never again be presented to us with the same ardent belief in their reality; and with them would depart most of the figures taken from Rabelaisian, medieval and Elizabethan sources which had appeared in the poems of Jack Lindsay and the earliest Slessor . . . symbols which had made a natural home for themselves in the paintings of Norman Lindsay but which needed to be assimilated at leisure before they could become (as they did in Slessor) a vital element in poetry. It was not a long step, really, from a "roaring pistol-boy" to Captain Cook, from a pirate to a navigator or an explorer; but it was, nevertheless, a step.

And round about 1930, if not in that precise year, there were published two books, one by Kenneth Slessor and one by Furnley Maurice, which significantly marked the changes that had occurred, and foreshadowed the developments that were to come. Slessor's "Five Visions of Captain Cook", first published in *Trio*, a limited edition, in 1929, was reprinted, along with "The Atlas", in *Cuckooz Contrey* in 1932. Part of the difference between *Cuckoo Contrey* and the Australian poetry which had preceded it might be seen in the wry, ironic, critical, essentially urban attitude to the Australian countryside shown in the small poem "Talbingo":

> That's what we're like out here,
> Beds of dried-up passions.

It was an attitude afterwards to be renewed in the satires of A. D. Hope and James McAuley. One could note, too, the change of outlook demonstrated in the subject of mermaids, where they are touched upon in "The Atlas". To Hugh McCrae—and rightly for his purposes—a mermaid would have been a serious matter; Slessor drily notes that such an apparition would have hardly been credible to the passengers of the P. & O. But it was in "Five Visions of Captain Cook" that the most dramatic break-through into the poetry of the twentieth century occurred; for this poem was to give much of the impetus to a whole series of "voyager poems" and explorer poems of great power and stature and significance. Robert D. FitzGerald's "Heemskerck Shoals" and "Between Two Tides", and probably also his convict poem "The Wind at Your Door"; Francis Webb's "A Drum for Ben Boyd", "Leichhardt in Theatre" and other narratives; William Hart-Smith's "Christopher Columbus": these and quite a few other major Australian poems may all conveniently (if not with complete accuracy; for FitzGerald, contemporaneously with Slessor, was finding his own way to the voyager poem) be dated from the first appearance of "Five Visions of Captain Cook".

An event which might conceivably have been of equal importance was the first publication in 1934 of Furnley Maurice's *Melbourne Odes*. Certainly, in New Zealand where I was then living, these poems, deriving from Carl Sandburg and Vachel Lindsay, seemed a very fierce, extravagant, and astonishingly "contemporary" kind of poetry; and in

Australia, by contrast with most of the verse then being written, the effect, so Professor Inglis Moore informs me, was no less remarkable. He himself had just returned from America and the Philippines, and Furnley Maurice seemed at that moment more alive than any of his contemporaries, a most exuberant phenomenon in the tranquil Australian scene. For some reason, perhaps because their looseness of form and uncertainty of style ultimately weakened their impact, the *Melbourne Odes* had no direct effect on the subsequent development of Australian poetry, and critical opinion has tended to ignore them. Yet at least we may say that in this volume Australian poetry burst with a vengeance into the urban world of the twentieth century; and broadly speaking, even if later poets have usually taken Auden for their guide, Furnley Maurice here pioneered the way.

Besides the voyager poems, and this break-through into the city, there have been a number of other movements after 1930 which should be mentioned.

There were the Angry Penguins, an advance guard group which vanished with a faint whiff of burnt feathers when it was found that one of their principal songsters, Ern Malley, was invented as a hoax by two poets, James McAuley and Harold Stewart, who disapproved of the obscurities practised by the Penguins.

There were the Jindyworobaks, led by Rex Ingamells and advocating an ardent nationalism in theme and idiom with special emphasis on the aborigines: a group without a great deal of significance because its members tended to disregard technique in favour of ideology, and because other poets, outside the movement, were already practising what the Jindyworobaks preached, but with more restraint.

There were the soldier poets of World War II. This is a group to which I have not been able to do full justice in this anthology: not from any belief that war is an unsuitable subject for poetry but simply because there were too many of

them, and most of them said essentially the same thing . . .
young men lifted beyond themselves by tremendous experi-
ence, and expressing their reaction in profoundly moving
elegy. A representative selection is included here; the rest
must be found in their own anthology, *Poets at War*, edited
by Ian Mudie and published in 1944.

There was, too, or so it was said by one prominent critic, a
Bulletin school of "minor nature poets" flourishing in the
forties . . . an observation in which, having had the privilege
of selecting the verse for the *Bulletin* at that period, I took a
peculiar and poignant interest.

In the fifties there were, said a distinguished visitor from
England (Mr J. M. D. Pringle in *Australian Accent*), two
rival schools of poetry: a nationalist school, and a "revolu-
tion" against this school led by A. D. Hope and James
McAuley whose themes were not so often concerned with
Australia and whose style, in contrast to the more Australian
idiom of the nationalists, was stricter and more classical. This,
though Mr Pringle afterwards qualified it, was partly true.

But poets cannot really be confined in these tidy categories,
any more than they can be imprisoned in a given period of
time. All talk about Movements means generalization, and
all generalizations are inaccurate. The fact that most of the
Angry Penguins practised obscurity and could be hoaxed by
it, does not prove that all were obscure or that none were
genuine poets: two at least of them have in fact survived to
write admirable (and perfectly clear) poetry. If the Jindy-
worobaks often ran to excess in their nationalism, neverthe-
less we must give them credit for inspiring many good poems
which, with better balance, made a highly effective use of the
ideas of the movement: William Hart-Smith's occasional poems
about the aborigines, some of Ian Mudie's Australiana, and Rol-
and Robinson's deeply felt poems of the bush. As for the
"minor nature poets" of the *Bulletin*, there were also the pierc-
ing and beautiful nature poems of David Campbell and Judith

Wright; there were the voyager poems of Francis Webb and
FitzGerald, which were neither minor nor concerned with
nature; and there were, simultaneously, Rosemary Dobson's ex-
quisite series of poems on medieval paintings which had noth-
ing specifically to do with nature or Australia. And as for the
two rival camps, national and classical—poets change, de-
velop, interchange ideas and vary their themes and styles far
too much for such a generalization ever to be wholly true.
If FitzGerald, having written some voyager poems, is a
"nationalist", he has also written about the trial of Warren
Hastings and the intrigues of Tongan chiefs, and we must
remember that "The Face of the Waters" is concerned not
with the origins of Australia but the origin of the universe.
If James McAuley, writing frequently on religious themes
and in a measured style, is in the "classical" camp, in what
company are we to place a simple nature poem such as "Late
Winter" or, considering its subject-matter, his long voyager
poem on Captain Quiros? In which school are we to place
the poems of Judith Wright, some of which are about Aus-
tralia, and some about love and metaphysics? Can we really
describe as "classical" the poems of A. D. Hope, so wild and
full of vehemence under the deceptive smoothness of his
style? The truth is, there is a place beyond the divisions of
the schools and movements where poetry meets; where it is
neither nationalist nor anti-nationalist, but poetry.

By and large, if we are to generalize, I think that what has
chiefly been going on in Australian poetry in this century is
a rediscovery and reassessment of the whole Australian en-
vironment: reaching back to the voyagers and explorers in
"Five Visions of Captain Cook" and "A Drum for Ben
Boyd"; exploring the more domestic mythology of convict
and landtaker in "The Wind at Your Door" and "Bullocky";
searching for the truths of the earth in the nature poems;
and extending to the analysis of urban and suburban life in
a variety of poems from *Melbourne Odes* to the satires of

A. D. Hope. Perhaps, except when writers have retreated into the ivory tower, the same thing can be said about the poetry of any country at any period: it is an exploration and a reassessment of its environment. But I think that in a new country it is something that happens with particular urgency.

It is really very difficult, once a country has thoroughly been explored by the poets of previous generations, to say anything new in poetry; and perhaps that is why, in England, poets as varied in their approach as T. S. Eliot and Dylan Thomas find themselves driven into obscurity and verbal experiment. Both, in their different ways, are searching for freshness. I remember once walking with John Cowper Powys through the village of Chaldon in Dorset. "Ah yes," he said as we left the old white-washed inn, *"Richard Garnett"*—Powys always talked in italics—"wrote a story about that." The old church as we passed it—"Ah, that's a *sinister* place! My brother *Theodore* wrote a story about that church." The great open country beyond the village, where Powys beat the grass with his walking stick in case the vipers bit him—"That's *Hardy's* moor!" . . . Well, where did one begin to write? What was there to say that had not already been said? I have never found any measuring stick whereby one could assess whether Australian poetry in recent years has been "better" or "worse" than that of England or America; but I do think that those who have written in this country in this century, having so much new subject-matter thrown open to them, have been lucky. We had heard about Henry the Fifth in poetry; we had not heard about Captain Cook. We had heard about the daffodil from Shakespeare and Herrick and Wordsworth; but nobody had heard about the wonga vine. It was as simple—and as exciting—as that.

I have no doubt that this newness, this feeling of discovery, has helped to produce some of the finest poetry that has been written in Australia in this century. But poetry (one really must admit) is not written exclusively in new countries. Or on new subjects. It is written on any subject, seen freshly and intensely; and there remain always, beyond new scenes and new patterns of living, the eternal truths and mysteries of human existence: the poetry of love, the poetry of metaphysics, the poetry of humanity. It is of no consequence at all that so noble and eloquent a poem as Hope's "An Epistle" should happen to be set in seventeenth century England while "The Wind at Your Door" is set at Parramatta; nor that "The Atlas" roves all over the world while "Five Bells" stays at home on Sydney Harbour. In the end—or in the beginning—it is the poetry that counts: whether it is beautiful, whether it is enjoyable . . . as, I trust, is the poetry in this anthology.

The poems are arranged, I should add, more or less in chronological order, according to the years of birth of the poets. This will give, roughly, a picture of the development of poetry in the period, but only roughly, for of course the year in which a poet was born is not the year in which he wrote any given poem. Since the picture could not be accurate, I have felt free to vary the order where it seemed desirable. "Country Towns", though some of the other poets were born earlier than Kenneth Slessor, was placed first because it is a pleasant and appropriate opening piece; and the curious surrealist poems of Randolph Stow are placed last, though Stow is not quite the youngest poet represented, because they seemed an intriguing note on which, for the time being, to end.

DOUGLAS STEWART

KENNETH SLESSOR

Country Towns

Country towns, with your willows and squares,
And farmers bouncing on barrel mares
To public-houses of yellow wood
With "1860" over their doors,
And that mysterious race of Hogans
Which always keeps General Stores. . . .

At the School of Arts, a broadsheet lies
Sprayed with the sarcasm of flies:
"The Great Golightly Family
Of Entertainers Here To-night"—
Dated a year and a half ago,
But left there, less from carelessness
Than from a wish to seem polite.

Verandas baked with musky sleep,
Mulberry faces dozing deep,
And dogs that lick the sunlight up
Like paste of gold—or, roused in vain
By far, mysterious buggy-wheels,
Lower their ears, and drowse again. . . .

Country towns with your schooner bees,
And locusts burnt in the pepper-trees,
Drown me with syrups, arch your boughs,
Find me a bench, and let me snore,
Till, charged with ale and unconcern,
I'll think it's noon at half-past four!

From *Five Visions of Captain Cook*

Flowers turned to stone! Not all the botany
Of Joseph Banks, hung pensive in a porthole,
Could find the Latin for this loveliness,

1

Could put the Barrier Reef in a glass box
Tagged by the horrid Gorgon squint
Of horticulture. Stone turned to flowers
It seemed—you'd snap a crystal twig,
One petal even of the water-garden,
And have it dying like a cherry-bough.

They'd sailed all day outside a coral hedge,
And half the night. Cook sailed at night,
Let there be reefs a fathom from the keel
And empty charts. The sailors didn't ask,
Nor Joseph Banks. Who cared? It was the spell
Of Cook that lulled them, bade them turn below,
Kick off their sea-boots, puff themselves to sleep,
Though there were more shoals outside
Than teeth in a shark's head. Cook snored loudest himself.

One day, a morning of light airs and calms,
They slid towards a reef that would have knifed
Their boards to mash, and murdered every man.
So close it sucked them, one wave shook their keel,
The next blew past the coral. Three officers,
In gilt and buttons, languidly on deck
Pointed their sextants at the sun. One yawned,
One held a pencil, one put eye to lens:
Three very peaceful English mariners
Taking their sights for longitude.
I've never heard
Of sailors aching for the longitude
Of shipwrecks before or since. It was the spell
Of Cook did this, the phylacteries of Cook.
Men who ride broomsticks with a mesmerist
Mock the typhoon. So, too, it was with Cook.

From *The Atlas*

I. THE KING OF CUCKOOZ

[*"The Platt of Argier and the Pts. adioining within the view thereof made by Robert Norton the Muster Mr. of his Ma't's Fleet ther Ao Di 1620 & by his owne carfull & dilligent observations then not without danger."*]

The King of Cuckooz Contrey
Hangs peaked above Argier
With Janzaries and Marabutts
To bid a sailor fear—

With lantern-eyed astrologers
Who walk upon the walls
And ram with stars their basilisks
Instead of cannon-balls.

And in that floating castle
(I tell you it is so)
Five thousand naked Concubines
With dulcimers do go.

Each rosy nose anoints a tile,
Bang, bang! the fort salutes,
When He, the King of Cuckooz Land,
Comes forth in satin boots,

Each rosy darling flies before
When he desires his tent,
Or, like a tempest driving flowers,
Inspects a battlement.

3

And this I spied by moonlight
Behind a royal bamboo—
That Monarch in a curricle
Which ninety virgins drew;

That Monarch drinking nectar
(Lord God, my tale attest!)
Milked from a snow-white elephant
As white as *your* white breast!

And this is no vain fable
As other knaves may lie—
Have I not got that Fowl aboard
Which no man may deny?

The King's own hunting-falcon
I limed across the side
When by the Bayes of Africa
King James's Fleet did ride.

What crest is there emblazoned,
Whose mark is this, I beg,
Stamped on the silver manacle
Around that dainty leg?

Let this be news to you, my dear,
How Man should be revered;
Though I'm no King of Cuckooz Land,
Behold as fierce a beard!

I have as huge an appetite,
As deep a kiss, my girl,
And *somewhere*, for the hand that seeks,
Perhaps a Sultan's pearl!

4

2. POST-ROADS

["*The Traveller's Guide, or A Most Exact Description of the Roads of England; being Mr. Ogilby's Actual Survey and Mensuration by the Wheel, &c.*"]

Post-roads that clapped with tympan heels
Of tilburies and whiskys rapidly spanking,
Where's now the tireless ghost of *Ogilby*?
Post-roads
That buoyed the rich and plunging springs
Of coaches vaster than Escurials,
Where now does *Ogilby* propel that Wheel,
What milestones does he pause to reprimand,
In what unmapped savanna of dumb shades?

Ye know not—ye are silent—brutish ducts
Numbed by the bastinadoes of iron boots,
Three hundred years asnore. Do you forget
The phaetons and fiacres, flys and breaks,
The world of dead men staring out of glass
That drummed upon your bones? Do you forget
Those nostrils oozing smoke, those floating tails,
Those criniers whipped with air?

And kidnapped lights,
Floats of rubbed yellow towed from window-panes,
Rushing their lozenges through headlong stones;
And smells of hackneys, mohair sour with damp,
Leather and slopped madeira, partridge-pies
Long-buried under floors; and yawning Fares
With bumping flap-dark spatulas of cards—
"Knave takes the ten . . . oh, God, I wish that it,
I wish that it was Guildford". . . .

5

Ogilby
Did not forget, could not escape such ecstacies,
Even in the monasteries of mensuration,
Could not forget the roads that he had gone
In fog and shining air. Each line was joy,
Each computation a beatitude,
A diagram of Ogilby's eye and ear
With soundings for the nose. Wherefore I think,

Wherefore I think some English gentleman,
Some learned doctor of the steak-houses,
Ending late dinner, having strolled outside
To quell the frivolous hawthorn, may behold
There in the moonshine, rolling up an hill,
Steered by no fleshly hand, with spokes of light,
The *Wheel—John Ogilby's Wheel*—the WHEEL hiss
    by,
Measuring mileposts of eternity.

3. DUTCH SEACOAST

[*"Toonneel der Steden van vereenighde Nederlanden met
hare Beschrijvingen uytgegeven by Joan. Blaeu."*]

No wind of Life may strike within
This little country's crystal bin,
Nor calendar compute the days
Tubed in their capsule of soft glaze.

Naked and rinsed, the bubble-clear
Canals of Amsterdam appear,
The blue-tiled turrets, china clocks
And glittering beaks of weathercocks.

A gulf of sweet and winking hoops
Whereon there ride 500 poops
With flying mouths and fleeting hair
Of saints hung up like candles there—

Fox-coloured mansions, lean and tall,
That burst in air but never fall,
Whose bolted shadows, row by row,
Float changeless on the stones below—

Sky full of ships, bay full of town,
A port of waters jellied brown:
Such is the world no tide may stir,
Sealed by the great cartographer.

O, could he but clap up like this
My decomposed metropolis,
Those other countries of the mind,
So tousled, dark and undefined!

4. MERMAIDS

["*A New and Accurat Map of the World, in two Hemispheres, Western and Eastern, with the Heavens and Elements, a Figure of the Spheare, the Eclipse of the Sunne, the Eclipse of the Moon.*"—J. Speed, 1675.]

Once Mermaids mocked your ships
With wet and scarlet lips
And fish-dark difficult hips, Conquistador;
Then Ondines danced with Sirens on the shore,
Then from his cloudy stall you heard the Kraken call,
And, mad with twisting flame, the Firedrake roar.

Such old-established Ladies
No mariner eyed askance,
But, coming on deck, would swivel his neck
To watch the darlings dance,
Or in the gulping dark of nights
Would cast his tranquil eyes
On singular kinds of Hermaphrodites
Without the least surprise.

Then portulano maps were scrolled
With compass-roses, green and gold,
That fired the stiff old Needle with their dyes
And wagged their petals over parchment skies.

Then seas were full of Dolphins' fins,
Full of swept bones and flying Jinns,
Beaches were filled with Anthropophagi
And Antient Africa with Palanquins.

Then sailors, with a flaked and rice-pale flesh
Staring from maps in sweet and poisoned places,
Diced the old Skeleton afresh
In brigs no bigger than their moon-bunched faces.

Those well-known and respected Harpies
Dance no more on the shore to and fro;
All that has ended long ago;
Nor do they sing outside the captain's porthole,
A proceeding fiercely reprehended
By the governors of the P. & O.

Nor do they tumble in the sponges of the moon
For the benefit of tourists in the First Saloon,
Nor fork their foaming lily-fins below the side
On the ranges of the ale-clear tide.

And scientists now, with binocular-eyes,
Remark in a tone of complacent surprise:
"Those pisciform mammals—pure Spectres, I fear—
Must be Doctor Gerbrandus's *Mermaids*, my dear!"

But before they can cause the philosopher trouble,
They are GONE like the cracking of a bubble.

Five Bells

Time that is moved by little fidget wheels
Is not my Time, the flood that does not flow.
Between the double and the single bell
Of a ship's hour, between a round of bells
From the dark warship riding there below,
I have lived many lives, and this one life
Of Joe, long dead, who lives between five bells.

Deep and dissolving verticals of light
Ferry the falls of moonshine down. Five bells
Coldly rung out in a machine's voice. Night and water
Pour to one rip of darkness, the Harbour floats
In air, the Cross hangs upside-down in water.

Why do I think of you, dead man, why thieve
These profitless lodgings from the flukes of thought
Anchored in Time? You have gone from earth,
Gone even from the meaning of a name;
Yet something's there, yet something forms its lips
And hits and cries against the ports of space,
Beating their sides to make its fury heard.

Are you shouting at me, dead man, squeezing your face
In agonies of speech on speechless panes?
Cry louder, beat the windows, bawl your name!

But I hear nothing, nothing . . . only bells,
Five bells, the bumpkin calculus of Time.
Your echoes die, your voice is dowsed by Life,
There's not a mouth can fly the pygmy strait—
Nothing except the memory of some bones
Long shoved away, and sucked away, in mud;
And unimportant things you might have done,
Or once I thought you did; but you forgot,
And all have now forgotten—looks and words
And slops of beer; your coat with buttons off,
Your gaunt chin and pricked eye, and raging tales
Of Irish kings and English perfidy,
And dirtier perfidy of publicans
Groaning to God from Darlinghurst.

Five bells.

Then I saw the road, I heard the thunder
Tumble, and felt the talons of the rain
The night we came to Moorebank in slab-dark,
So dark you bore no body, had no face,
But a sheer voice that rattled out of air
(As now you'd cry if I could break the glass),
A voice that spoke beside me in the bush,
Loud for a breath or bitten off by wind,
Of Milton, melons, and the Rights of Man,
And blowing flutes, and how Tahitian girls
Are brown and angry-tongued, and Sydney girls
Are white and angry-tongued, or so you'd found.
But all I heard was words that didn't join
So Milton became melons, melons girls,
And fifty mouths, it seemed, were out that night,
And in each tree an Ear was bending down,
Or something had just run, gone behind grass,
When, blank and bone-white, like a maniac's thought,
The naphtha-flash of lightning slit the sky,

Knifing the dark with deathly photographs.
There's not so many with so poor a purse
Or fierce a need, must fare by night like that,
Five miles in darkness on a country track,
But when you do, that's what you think.

Five bells.

In Melbourne, your appetite had gone,
Your angers too; they had been leeched away
By the soft archery of summer rains
And the sponge-paws of wetness, the slow damp
That stuck the leaves of living, snailed the mind,
And showed your bones, that had been sharp with rage,
The sodden ecstasies of rectitude.
I thought of what you'd written in faint ink,
Your journal with the sawn-off lock, that stayed behind
With other things you left, all without use,
All without meaning now, except a sign
That someone had been living who now was dead:
"At Labassa. Room 6 x 8
On top of the tower; because of this, very dark
And cold in winter. Everything has been stowed
Into this room—500 books all shapes
And colours, dealt across the floor
And over sills and on the laps of chairs;
Guns, photoes of many differant things
And differant curioes that I obtained. . . ."

In Sydney, by the spent aquarium-flare
Of penny gaslight on pink wallpaper,
We argued about blowing up the world,
But you were living backward, so each night
You crept a moment closer to the breast,
And they were living, all of them, those frames
And shapes of flesh that had perplexed your youth,

And most your father, the old man gone blind,
With fingers always round a fiddle's neck,
That graveyard mason whose fair monuments
And tablets cut with dreams of piety
Rest on the bosoms of a thousand men
Staked bone by bone, in quiet astonishment
At cargoes they had never thought to bear,
These funeral-cakes of sweet and sculptured stone.

Where have you gone? The tide is over you,
The turn of midnight water's over you,
As Time is over you, and mystery,
And memory, the flood that does not flow.
You have no suburb, like those easier dead
In private berths of dissolution laid—
The tide goes over, the waves ride over you
And let their shadows down like shining hair,
But they are Water; and the sea-pinks bend
Like lilies in your teeth, but they are Weed;
And you are only part of an Idea.
I felt the wet push its black thumb-balls in,
The night you died, I felt your eardrums crack,
And the short agony, the longer dream,
The Nothing that was neither long nor short;
But I was bound, and could not go that way,
But I was blind, and could not feel your hand.
If I could find an answer, could only find
Your meaning, or could say why you were here
Who now are gone, what purpose gave you breath
Or seized it back, might I not hear your voice?

I looked out of my window in the dark
At waves with diamond quills and combs of light
That arched their mackerel-backs and smacked the sand
In the moon's drench, that straight enormous glaze,

And ships far off asleep, and Harbour-buoys
Tossing their fireballs wearily each to each,
And tried to hear your voice, but all I heard
Was a boat's whistle, and the scraping squeal
Of seabirds' voices far away, and bells,
Five bells. Five bells coldly ringing out.

Five bells.

Beach Burial

Softly and humbly to the Gulf of Arabs
The convoys of dead sailors come;
At night they sway and wander in the waters far under,
But morning rolls them in the foam.

Between the sob and clubbing of the gunfire
Someone, it seems, has time for this,
To pluck them from the shallows and bury them in burrows
And tread the sand upon their nakedness;

And each cross, the driven stake of tidewood,
Bears the last signature of men,
Written with such perplexity, with such bewildered pity,
The words choke as they begin—

"*Unknown seaman*"—the ghostly pencil
Wavers and fades, the purple drips,
The breath of the wet season has washed their inscriptions
As blue as drowned men's lips,

Dead seamen, gone in search of the same landfall,
Whether as enemies they fought,
Or fought with us, or neither; the sand joins them together,
Enlisted on the other front.

El Alamein

From *The Victoria Markets Recollected in Tranquillity*

I

Winds are bleak, stars are bright,
Loads lumber along the night:
Looming, ghastly white,
A towering truck of cauliflowers sways
Out of the dark, roped over and packed tight
Like faces of a crowd of football jays.

The roads come in, roads dark and long,
To the knock of hubs and a sleepy song.
Heidelberg, Point Nepean, White Horse,
Flemington, Keilor, Dandenong,
Into the centre from the source.

Rocking in their seats
The worn-out drivers droop
When dawn stirs in the streets
And the moon's a silver hoop;
Come rumbling into the silent mart,
To put their treasure at its heart,
Waggons, lorries, a lame Ford bus,
Like ants along the arms of an octopus
Whose body is all one mouth; that pays them hard
And drives them back with less than a slave's reward.

When Batman first at Heaven's command
Said, "This is the place for a peanut-stand,"
It must have been grand!

II

"Cheap today, lady; cheap today!"
Jostling water-melons roll
From fountains of Earth's mothering soul.

Tumbling from box and tray
Rosy, cascading apples play
Each with a glowing aureole
Caught from a split sun-ray.
"Cheap today, lady, cheap today."
Hook the carcasses from the dray!
(*Where the dun bees hunt in droves*
Apples ripen in the groves.)

An old horse broods in a Chinaman's cart
While from the throbbing mart
Go cheese and celery, pears and jam
In barrow, basket, bag, or pram
To the last dram the purse affords—
Food, food for the hordes!

Shuffling in the driven crush
The souls and the bodies cry,
Rich and poor, skimped and flush,
"Spend or perish, buy or die!"

Food, food for the hordes!
Turksheads tumble on the boards.

There's honey at the dairy produce stall
Where the strung saveloys festooning fall;
Yielding and yellow, the beautiful butter blocks
Confront the poultryman's plucked Plymouth Rocks.
The butcher is gladly selling,
Chopping and slaughtering, madly yelling.
A bull-like bellow for captured sales;
A great crowd surges around his scales.
Slap down the joint!
The finger point
Wobbles and comes alive,
Springs round to twenty and back to five.

No gracious burbling, nor arts to please,
No hypocritical felicities.
Buy and be damned to you! Sell and be damned also!
Decry the goods, he'll tell you where to go!

To him Creation's total aim
Is selling chops to a doubting dame.
And what will matter his steaks and joints,
The underdone and the overdone,
On the day when old Earth jumps the points
And swings into the sun?

Along the shadows, furtive, lone,
The unwashed terrier carries his week-end bone.
An old horse with a pointed hip
And dangling disillusioned under-lip
Stands in a harvest-home of cabbage-leaves
And grieves.
A lady by a petrol case,
With a far-off wounded look in her face
Says, in a voice of uncertain pitch,
"Muffins", or "crumpets", I'm not sure which.
A pavement battler whines with half a sob,
"Ain't anybody got a bloody bob?"
Haunted by mortgages and overdrafts
The old horse droops between the shafts.
A smiling Chinaman upends a bag
And spills upon the bench with thunder-thud
(A nearby urchin trilling the newest rag)
Potatoes caked with loamy native mud.
Andean pinnacles of labelled jam.
The melting succulence of two-toothed lamb.
The little bands of hemp that truss
The succulent asparagus

That stands like tiny sheaves of purple wheat
Ready to eat!
Huge and alluring hams and rashered swine
In circular repetitive design.
Gobbling turkeys and ducks in crates,
Pups in baskets and trays of eggs;
A birdman turns and gloomily relates
His woes to a girl with impossible legs.

When Batman first at Heaven's command
Stuck flag-staffs in this sacred strand . . .
We'll leave all that to the local band.

Rabbits skinned in a pink nude row,
Little brown kidneys out on show;
"Ready for the pot, mum, ready to bake!"
Buy them, devour them for pity's sake—
(*Trapped, 'neath the moon in a field of dream,*
Did anyone hear a bunny scream?)

"Cheap to-day, lady, cheap to-day."
Slimy fish slide off the tray.
Women pondering with a sigh—
"Spend or perish, buy or die!"
Packed with babies and Brussels sprouts,
It's a ricketty pram for a woman to shove—
But tell me, lady, whereabouts
Is the long leisure of love?

Flattened out on a trestle board
Somebody's trousers await their lord.

.   .   .   .   .   .

IV

Shuffling in the driven tide
The huddled people press,
Hoarding and gloating, having defied
Hunger, cold and nakedness
For a few days more—or less.
Is it nothing to you that pass?
Will you not pity their need?
Store beef fattens on stolen grass,
Brows grow dark with covetous greed,
Storm or manacle, cringe or pray,
There is no way but the money way.

Pouring suns, pouring heavens, pouring earth,
And the life-giving seas:
Treasure eternally flowing forth,
None greater than these!
Richness, colour and form,
Ripe flavours and juices rare!

Within men's hearts rises a deathless prayer
Deep as a spirit storm,
Giving thanks that the earth has offered such
(So grateful to the eye, so rich to touch)
Miraculous varieties of fare.

And yet that lamb with the gentle eye,
She had to die. . . .
There have been foolish dreams
Of fishes pulled from reedy streams,
Of delicate earthly fruits
Being torn up by the roots—
But only the Mandragora screams.
Gentle curates and slaughtermen

Murder the cattle in the pen:
Body, Spirit, the Word, the Breath
Only survive by so much death.
The old horse with the pointed hip
And disillusioned under-lip
Stands in a drift of cabbage-leaves
And grieves.

There is no wile to capture
Rugged and massive things
In all their fervent rapture
Soaring without wings.

. . . . . .

Grace is the power:
Only vision can flower
Into immortal song.
Art is mannered, pure and long—
These folk, accursed, can have no vital part
In schooled philosophies or templed art.
A force that throngs the by-ways and the streets
A dark, enormous influence that pours
Its passion through the light and vainly beats
On spired churches and closed college doors.
In love—the jealous pistol and the "jug",
In hate—the bottle-swinger and the thug,
In peace—some rows of figures and a graph,
In war—a motto on a cenotaph.

Now the plough is in the shed,
And old Nugget paws his bed.
   Steal away,
   Gentle day;
Apples, ripen for the dray!

19

The Apple-tree

A maiden sat in an apple-tree,
Oh, and the blossoms round her!
A maiden sat in an apple-tree,
'Twas there that I found her,
'Twas there, in a dapple of sun,
In a smother of snowflake petals,
I saw her swinging
Her feet and singing
"One, two, three—one, two, three—one,
Two, three",
To the fall of the apple petals:
Ah, me!

The maiden, she had laughing eyes,
And her frock was like a cloud,
And the voice of her was like her eyes,
And softer than a cloud,
And over me came sudden spell,
Hearing the falling "one-two-three"
Of the maiden's counting
And the snowflakes mounting
At the foot of the apple-tree;
One fell,
Two fell, and three, and the spell on me;
Ah, well!

A shudder ran like a run of wind
Over the apple-tree; she
Felt the wind, but only a wind
Stirring the apple-tree;
It was the wind of life
Trimming the spring; what but summer's breath
Taking the swinging

Feet and singing—
"One, two, three—one, two, three—one, two—death!"

Oh, spring,
To maid of the flowering apple-breath
Clinging!

The Net Menders

I came upon them by a strip of sea,
In a drizzle of rain mending their fishing-net,
Four swift brown hands, and lean with industry,
Shuttling the thin twine skilfully in-out, repairing the fret
Of rock-jag, shark-tooth and thresh;
He, tense as a mackerel, strong and agile,
Sea-eyed and grim as a rock, turned, and his smile
Was as the wonder of sunshine on sea-rock,
His fingers harping the net-mesh;
She on the sea-side, facing the land, took stock
Of me leisurely nearing, through half-shut eyes.
"Defence," I thought; but her mouth relaxed, went sweet
And soft as a sea-flower, her hands' enterprise
On the sea-side of the breaks in the net
Rippling the strings of the two-sided harp o' the sea,
And I thought, "Here is where sea-melodies meet,
Mending the breakage of earth-and-sea-fret,"
And the strange great grace of simplicity came on me.

If they had angers in them, these two by the sea,
Not in the two days dwelt with them,
Watching the shuttle flying, the flat corks tied,
And the strong boat pitch-caulked for battle with the sea,
Was flaw apparent in the gem;
Their poverty, too real for pride to hide,
Gave them no envy, not even in the lamp-light

And shadows of our talk,
Not when the net was trailed and netted nought
Save weed, nor when I spoke, that unforgettable night
We fought the tide, and drifted home star-caught,
And I spoke of the hawk
Now in the dark vanished, that all day long
Circled and soared and plunged on innocence; "Cruel life!"
    I cried
But my cry crossed over the woman's song,
Over the zither of the boat cutting the brine, and died,
And the man said, "It is life,"
And the boat gritted the waiting sand
With sound of a cleansing knife,
And we slept, at life's command.

ETHEL ANDERSON

Waking, Child, While You Slept
(From "Bucolic Eclogues")

Waking, child, while you slept, your mother took
Down from its wooden peg her reaping-hook,
Rustless with use, to cut (her task when dawn
With nervous light would bead the dusky leaves)
From the cold wheat-paddock's shivering fringe, two sheaves;
Against a block she'd thrash the golden grain,
Then winnow corn and husk, and toss again . . . .
With bustling care, in genial haste, not late
Her cows she'd milk, her butter churn, and set
Fresh cream in scalded pans. Her hens she'd feed
With hot scraps, stirred in pollard from the bin;
Then give her dribbling calves what drink they need;
Or drive with flowery staff
Meek stragglers through the gate;

22

Or on her youngest-born
Impose the fret,
The letter'd tyranny, of the alphabet.

To dig, to delve, to drive wild cattle in,
("Ester, ley thou thy mekeness al a-doun")
To scour, to sweep, to wash and iron, to spin;
("Penalopee and Marcia Catoun
Make of your wifehood no comparisoun,")
To sew, to darn, to cook, to bake, to brew,
To bear, to rear, to nurse her children, too;
("And Cleopatre, with al thy passioun
Hyde ye your trouthe of love, and your renoun.")

Though, child, your mother, trembling, smiled at fear,
Fears had she; the blackfellow's cruel spear,
White desperadoes. When to the open well
She crept at nightfall, being all alone,
For comfort, then, she'd watch her frugal rush,
The only gleam in all that virgin bush,
Cheer the unshutter'd, distant window-pane;
Then hoist her twirling bucket yet again.

When in a drought the waterholes ran dry
And of "dry-bible" half the herds would die,
And others in their agony creep to lie
About the homestead, moaning piteously,
Or, famished, on the deadly purple weed,
Or poisonous variegated thistle, feed,
The men being absent, then, to give release,
She brought to every suffering brute death's peace;
     Who never heard the rain
     Fall, but she heard again
     The cattle in their pain.

But in a lucky year your mother's care
Was all to save the wealth her orchard bore;
Apples and plums, peach, apricot and pear,
Mandarins, nectarines, tangerines, a score
Of rosy berries, currants and their kind;
Drying these last, through muslin she would squeeze
Damson or apple cheese;
Quinces, conserve; bottle black mulberries . . . .

She for her cellar with a cheerful mind
Would brew in tubs peach-beer,
Sparkling and clear,
Rub pears, and trinities of apples bruise
To perry and cider in a wooden cruse.
Of keeving and pomace then gossip ran,
One servant assigned her being a Devon man,
Whose convict clothes and homely face—so kind—
Smiling, you may remember, musing on
The knight, his grandson, and the judge, his son.

Kunai-mai-pa Mo

Into the shadow Kunai-mai-pa Mo
Would go, would go.

His mother tied his wrists with strings
"In case," said she, "they turn to wings.

"If Mo flew away, I'd daub my heart with clay,
With blue clay, yellow clay, the day Mo flew away."

But Kunai-mai-pa Mo
Would go, would go.

His mother wept. With many sighs
She made a necklace of his thighs,

Put his bleached finger-tip
Sadly through her upper lip,

Eat, charm of greatest worth,
Hibiscus flowers in earth.

Nothing else left to do,
She sawed three fingers through

And much afraid, much afraid,
Followed Mo through the shade.

J. ALEX. ALLAN

Breaking

(Greece—1941)

Where shall I hide my head and my face?
The rocks are about me: between them
I have wormed and lie prone,
While over me, sheering through shot-riddled space,
Engined vultures of doom—I have seen them—
Swoop avidly, peer, and depart.
My heart is as cold as the stone
Which shelters my dread and my heart!
I know, while I cower, the fear of the fox
Cut off from his earth by the hounds of the pack—
The fear of the coney turned doubling back
To the hope of a hold in the rocks!
How long since I scrambled and lay—
A year—or a day?

I am fighting the terror that laps
My bones and my body in ice!
A tremor of prayer, perhaps . . .
A whisper to Him—would a whisper suffice?

(For the ghost of a sound would betray me!)
"I have lifted up mine eyes . . ."
"Father, God, I shall arise—"
"Now I lay me—now I lay me . . ."
Vain but all I know—
Shreds of things I used to patter,
Lost—forgotten—(will it matter?)
Years and years ago!

. . . . . .

High on the hillside the thread of a road
Climbs down to the pass; and below me
The utter ravine!
Far east, in the hamlet, the faces that glowed
At twilight, in doorways, to know me,
Shall know me not ever: they lie
Where the shocked olives listen and lean,
Black, twisted, and turned to the sky.
The charred faggots shrink from their bomb-splintered
    hearth,
The Christ at the cross-roads hangs cleft on the Cross,
The greybeard lies clutching two handfuls of moss,
The goatherd sprawls torn in the garth;
And Godhead and beauty are trampled in mud
And blackness and blood!

The death that strikes slantingly down,
The shrieking crescendo therefrom,
Rent earth and wrecked waggon bestrown
With the spattering vomit that spouts from the bomb!
Machine-guns that cackle and slaughter. . . .

. . . . . .

Rede me, time and space and sun—
Shall I meet that flute-voiced one,
Old Larissa's dove-eyed daughter?
Or, far out to south,
Where our breaths were wont to mingle,
Lies she dead athwart the ingle—
Blood upon her mouth?

. . . . . .

Hunted and breaking, alone with the dead—
Where shall I hide my face and my head?

HARLEY MATTHEWS

The Return of the Native

I have come back again.
Back to the one thing I have met
Worth loving—You.
Yes, I know that now, hearing
That bird who, just returned at this time, too,
Cries out there in the clearing.
The rain-bird he is called by farmers: Yet
It's not because he brings
Even a drizzle when, year after year
He comes and prophesies the springs.
But they remember how they hear
His voice complaining,
Full of some brighter place he can't forget,
Perched alone on a fence-post when it's raining.

And we will hear him in the night
Too, crying for his distant sun,
"Me. Me. Poor me. Me."—His notes run
On, on to a sad silence.

27

When he's gone
Hence, at our summer's end, will his song be
Still in that minor key,
Voicing the same nostalgic pain?
Do not ask me.
The answer's in a land from us remote.
All I can say, and on a major note
Is—I am home again.

PETER HOPEGOOD

Dithyramb in Retrospect

I was carried to a font.
Stranger fingers marked my front.
 Significant, no doubt, the rite
 that day was day and night was night:
 yet it could not make me see.
 Lifeless was that sorcery.

Then I sought a font in Toil,
smeared my sweaty brow with Soil.
 Still by fingers strange 'twas done,
 though the fingers were my own.

Then I sought a font in Fire;
leapt I Armageddon's pyre.
 Iron set on me his hand:
 but 'twas still a stranger brand.

Then a passion smote my heart
with a devastating dart.
 Still I could in nowise see.
 Darkness ever compassed me.

With my pain I face the Sky
when my planet there must ply . . .
    and the fingers of the Wind
    touch me with my Very Wand,
    Straightway know I power to see
    what the light has hid from me.
    By the Wind that walks the Night
    I am baptized into sight.

The Protagonist

No sleep! I rise and burn the night away.
Swift through the open window drives a moth—
and stages yet another Passion Play.

The candle flares—a Star is in the east.
The altar's lit for sacrifice afresh,
the dance of death and ecstasy, the feast,
more bread than wine, of bloodless insect flesh.

Sudden, the reckless Dionysian whirl
is ended in a headlong plummet dive—
Descended into Hell—Now mark the curl,
the crisped and singed antennae ends contrive.
The devotee aswoon, as in the grave,
lies two untroubled seconds. Then, it stirs—
He rose the third day—see, the struggle brave
resumes—the palsied wing yet feebly whirrs!
The painful upward crawl that gathers strength
and speed betimes—*ascended into Heaven*—
the pause in ecstasy, a thumbnail's length
below the Flame, the quickening flesh to leaven
at life's own Source . . . *He sitteth at the right
hand of*—that beauteous, quivering naked Gleam.

Desires resurge. So keen the new delight,
all the old scorching pain becomes a dream:
the insistent Present calls; the Past forgot,
once more the Living Bread prepares the Feast;
the Hero-victim re-enacts the Plot—
the candle flares. A Star is in the east.

PAUL GRANO

"A New Shirt!" Why?

"A new shirt!" Why?
I have a shirt—two—three!
worn a bit, not many days to them,
nor perhaps to me.

Soon earth'll have one of them,
my body in it,
and later an end
to their identities. Quit

wholly the shirt's and no resurrection!
And the body's? What date,
and will it ask covering?
Let a new shirt wait

convention's ultimate need.
Much else the money buys
that may go with me
when my body dies.

My body dead, and I
senseless of the teaching Five,
suffering strange converse,
would you have me strive

with my lustrous Mentor
eager to assert
"Sir, in the sun time
I remember a shirt"?

or would you not prefer
me to recall
a day on Coot-tha
when we saw fall

from furnaced clouds
rain sifting down
like golden ash
on Brisbane Town;

or of a certain night
make cry:
"Sir, there was a coffee shop
and there my friend and I

sat in the far corner
of the chattering scene
elate with the fragrance
and bright bitterness of the bean,

great thoughts within us
and by the lips of each,
not we, but the vital dead
making high speech.

A new . . . We'll to the bookshop
where small money buys
the richest minds or out to Ashgrove's
twisted creek, there belly-wise,

to watch the ants lumping
(how manlike!) each its load of dirt
up sheer blade cliffs and down—
and forget the shirt.

MAX DUNN

I Danced Before I Had Two Feet

I danced before I had two feet
And sang before I had a tongue;
I laughed before I had two eyes
And loved before my heart was young.

I swam before I had two hands
And held the distance in my toes
Before I heard the stars or knew
The wild compulsion of the rose.

I bore the fruit of many lives
Before I came into this day;
I knew before my grave was made
The worms eat only death away.

ERNEST G. MOLL

Eagles Over the Lambing Paddock

The business of the lambing ewes would make me
At times a trifle sick. The strain and quiver
Of life just squeezed past death to stand and shiver
Wet in the cold on wobbly legs would shake me
With pity for these accidents of lust,
Sometimes with mere disgust.

But I would watch the wedge-tailed eagle wheeling
In skies as biting blue as ocean spaces,
Great wing above the messy commonplaces
Of birth and death and the weak sprawl of feeling;
And coolly then would flow through heart and brain
Respect for life again.

A Gnarled Riverina Gum-tree

Knob and hump upon this tree
And the humpy things in me
Have a greeting for each other
And a word I think is "brother".

Straighter trees there are that shake
The very heavens wide awake,
And straighter souls, yes, many a one,
Than mine keep threatening the sun.

They speed on without a word
Or the brief rapture of a bird,
Fearful lest the sky might shut
Like iron doors above them. But

I the man and this wried wood,
Hump to hump, as old friends should,
Squat and talk and watch them run
Stretched up thin to catch the sun.

T. INGLIS MOORE

Star Drill

Comfort me with stars, not apples,
For always the sky was my bright consoler.
Tonight I am reconciled to aching feet
Seeing the lights of heaven themselves,

33

Obedient to reveille blown by sunset,
Go equably marching, in humble squad-drill,
Across the viewless bull-ring of time,
Keeping their constellated ranks,
Never breaking line, falling out of step,
Treading on heels of Mars or Mercury.

Even Orion and the Eagle form threes.
Even comets, lighting a curve across space,
Are only doing, perhaps, a centennial double,
Or a cometary P.T. to a soundless
"Arms bend! Tails ex-tend!"

Earth is manifesto of a million commandings:
Fixed trees moving sunward at the light's law,
The far moon conscripting the great tides,
Svelte tigers preying, and bees homing,
Submissive to ancient, primal commands
Passed down through instinctive ages,
With man, too, no less creature of compulsion,
His mind obedient to superior blood,
Saluting, unconsciously, the cloaked desires.
All life obeys orderings.

Why should I, earth's manikin, rebel
At being a soldier along with marching suns,
One with the invincible armies of heaven?
But where are the drums that time their feet?
Who is the shouting astral sergeant?
Who the celestial C.O.?

Comrade in Arms

Brew your potion, mix your spell,
Pestle in mortar pound, then tell
How the power of your chemic art
Captured and kept my Romany heart!

What volcanic draught of fire
Loosed the lava of desire
Still unquenched, a hidden flood
Flowing, flowing down my blood,
Bursting all the jealous weirs
Built by time across the years?
What alembic wrought the charms
Holding me in your white arms?
Wife and comrade, mate and friend,
Yours I am until the end;
We have conquered life, though death
Take joint glory from our breath.

Lithe of limb and fine of heart,
Thoroughbred in every part,
So you win, by double grace,
Flesh and mind to your embrace.
Cool, broad brow and pool-brown eyes
Guard your gentleness, and wise
Innocence whose morning zest
No day undews, no evening west
Darkens; warm your gloryings
In each loveliness that sings
Clear from bird and tree and flower;
Deep your passion in the hour
Sacramental, when our lips
Seal the intrusive world's eclipse.

Ever on my wounds you laid
Balsam of understanding, made
Faith unflecked a potent balm
Saving me from each dark harm.
Greater even than all these
Glows your courage, that decrees
How together we can face,

Hand in hand, war's doom, and brace
Shoulders to carry swags whose weight
Bulks with pain and doubts of fate,
Knowing yet the strong content
From answering the high event.

ROBERT D. FitzGERALD

Back from the Paved Way

Back from the paved way this night is met
by the sea's lost children. A lamp's rivulet
streams over a brown body, a red sash;
for who walks here walks as a rainbow-splash
upon a curtain of jet.

Flowers in stiff hair; broad teeth, white-gleaming; black eyes,
smooth but still savage, caught in a molten flash;
the oiled skins; the rapt singing; the soft tongue:
be these remembered until memory dies!
And though I have known these people near their true core
in further, untroubled villages hid among
remote, rain-shattering hills where their lives make
no count of the years passing, I think of them more
here, pressed against a new meaning, a strange mode
unparalleled in the old path they forsake.

For here their steel must sharpen on harsh files
(race grinding race) to cleave now a fresh road;
else shall they tread the sunlight some few miles,
then, singing even with last bitter breath,
go decked in paper garlands down to death.

Fusion of bloods, submergence of past things,
eclipse, survival—it's tomorrow's care!
Dark Loma behind her lattice flicks the strings
and the tune steps out light-footed upon the air.

ROBERT D. FITZGERALD

The Face of the Waters

Once again the scurry of feet—those myriads
crossing the black granite; and again
laughter cruelly in pursuit; and then
the twang like a harpstring or the spring of a trap,
and the swerve on the polished surface: the soft little pads
sidling and skidding and avoiding; but soon caught up
in the hand of laughter and put back. . . .

There is no release from the rack
of darkness for the unformed shape,
the unexisting thought
stretched half-and-half
in the shadow of beginning and that denser black
under the imminence of huge pylons—
the deeper nought;
but neither is there anything to escape,
or to laugh,
or to twang that string which is not a string but silence
plucked at the heart of silence.

Nor can there be a floor to the bottomless;
except in so far as conjecture must arrive,
lungs cracking, at the depth of its dive;
where downward further is further distress
with no change in it; as if a mile and an inch
are equally squeezed into a pinch,
and retreating limits of cold mind
frozen, smoothed, defined.

Out of the tension of silence (the twanged string);
from the agony of not being (that terrible laughter
tortured by darkness); out of it all

37

once again the tentative migration; once again
a universe on the edge of being born:
feet running fearfully out of nothing
at the core of nothing:
colour, light, life, fearfully
becoming eyes and understanding: sound becoming ears....

For eternity is not space reaching
on without end to it; not time without end to it,
nor infinity working round in a circle;
but a placeless dot enclosing nothing,
the pre-time pinpoint of impossible beginning,
enclosed by nothing, not even by emptiness—
impossible: so wholly at odds with possibilities
that, always emergent and wrestling and interlinking
they shatter it and return to it, are all of it and part of it.
It is your hand stretched out to touch your neighbour's,
and feet running through the dark, directionless like dark-
    ness.

Worlds that were spun adrift re-enter
that intolerable centre;
indeed the widest looping comet
never departed from it;
it alone exists.
And though, opposing it, there persists
the enormous structure of forces, laws,
as background for other coming and going,
that's but a pattern, a phase, no pause,
of ever-being-erected, ever-growing
ideas unphysically alternative
to nothing, which is the quick. You may say hills live,
or life's the imperfect aspect of a flowing
that sorts itself as hills; much as thoughts wind
selectively through mind.

The egg-shell collapses
in the fist of the eternal instant;
all is what it was before.
Yet is that eternal instant
the pinpoint bursting into reality,
the possibilities and perhapses,
the feet scurrying on the floor.
It is the suspense also
with which the outward thrust
holds the inward surrender—
the stresses in the shell before it buckles under:
the struggle to magpie-morning and all life's clamour and
    lust;
the part breaking through the whole;
light and the clear day and so simple a goal.

The Wind at Your Door

(To Mary Gilmore)

My ancestor was called on to go out—
a medical man, and one such must by law
wait in attendance on the pampered knout
and lend his countenance to what he saw,
lest the pet, patting with too bared a claw,
be judged a clumsy pussy. Bitter and hard,
see, as I see him, in that jailhouse yard.

Or see my thought of him: though time may keep
elsewhere tradition or a portrait still,
I would not feel under his cloak of sleep
if beard there or smooth chin, just to fulfill
some canon of precision. Good or ill
his blood's my own; and scratching in his grave
could find me more than I might wish to have.

Let him then be much of the middle style
of height and colouring; let his hair be dark
and his eyes green; and for that slit, the smile
that seemed inhuman, have it cruel and stark,
but grant it could be too the ironic mark
of all caught in the system—who the most,
the doctor or the flesh twined round that post?

There was a high wind blowing on that day;
for one who would not watch, but looked aside,
said that when twice he turned it blew his way
splashes of blood and strips of human hide
shaken out from the lashes that were plied
by one right-handed, one left-handed tough,
sweating at this paid task, and skilled enough.

That wind blows to your door down all these years.
Have you not known it when some breath you drew
tasted of blood? Your comfort is in arrears
of just thanks to a savagery tamed in you
only as subtler fears may serve in lieu
of thong and noose—old savagery which has built
your world and laws out of the lives it spilt.

For what was jailyard widens and takes in
my country. Fifty paces of stamped earth
stretch; and grey walls retreat and grow so thin
that towns show through and clearings—new raw birth,
which burst from handcuffs—and free hands go forth
to win tomorrow's harvest from a vast
ploughland—the fifty paces of that past.

But see it through a window barred across,
from cells this side, facing the outer gate
which shuts on freedom, opens on its loss

in a flat wall. Look left now through the grate
at buildings like more walls, roofed with grey slate
or hollowed in the thickness of laid stone
each side the court where the crowd stands this noon.

One there with the officials, thick of build,
not stout, say burly (so this obstinate man
ghosts in the eyes) is he whom enemies killed
(as I was taught) because the monopolist clan
found him a grit in their smooth-turning plan,
too loyally active on behalf of Bligh.
So he got lost; and history passed him by.

But now he buttons his long coat against
the biting gusts, or as a gesture of mind,
habitual; as if to keep him fenced
from stabs of slander sticking him from behind,
sped by the schemers never far to find
in faction, where approval from one source
damns in another clubroom as of course.

This man had Hunter's confidence, King's praise;
and settlers on the starving Hawkesbury banks
recalled through twilight drifting across their days
the doctor's fee of little more than thanks
so often; and how sent by their squeezed ranks
he put their case in London. I find I lack
the hateful paint to daub him wholly black.

Perhaps my life replies to his too much
through veiling generations dropped between.
My weakness here, resentments there, may touch
old motives and explain them, till I lean
to the forgiveness I must hope may clean
my own shortcomings; since no man can live
in his own sight if it will not forgive.

Certainly I must own him whether or not
it be my will. I was made understand
this much when once, marking a freehold lot,
my papers suddenly told me it was land
granted to Martin Mason. I felt his hand
heavily on my shoulder, and knew what coil
binds life to life through bodies, and soul to soil.

There, over to one corner, a bony group
of prisoners waits; and each shall be in turn
tied by his own arms in a human loop
about the post, with his back bared to learn
the price of seeking freedom. So they earn
three hundred rippling stripes apiece, as set
by the law's mathematics against the debt.

These are the Irish batch of Castle Hill,
rebels and mutineers, my countrymen
twice over: first, because of those to till
my birthplace first, hack roads, raise roofs; and then
because their older land time and again
enrolls me through my forbears; and I claim
as origin that threshold whence we came.

One sufferer had my surname, and thereto
"Maurice", which added up to history once;
an ignorant dolt, no doubt, for all that crew
was tenantry. The breed of clod and dunce
makes patriots and true men: could I announce
that Maurice as my kin I say aloud
I'd take his irons as heraldry, and be proud.

Maurice is at the post. Its music lulls,
one hundred lashes done. If backbone shows
then play the tune on buttocks! But feel his pulse;

that's what a doctor's for; and if it goes
lamely, then dose it with these purging blows—
which have not made him moan; though, writhing there,
"Let my neck be," he says, "and flog me fair."

One hundred lashes more, then rest the flail.
What says the doctor now? "This dog won't yelp;
he'll tire you out before you'll see him fail;
here's strength to spare; go on!" Ay, pound to pulp;
yet when you've done he'll walk without your help,
and knock down guards who'd carry him being bid,
and sing no song of where the pikes are hid.

It would be well if I could find, removed
through generations back—who knows how far?—
more than a surname's thickness as a proved
bridge with that man's foundations. I need some star
of courage from his firmament, a bar
against surrenders: faith. All trials are less
than rain-blacked wind tells of that old distress.

Yet I can live with Mason. What is told
and what my heart knows of his heart, can sort
much truth from falsehood, much there that I hold
good clearly or good clouded by report;
and for things bad, ill grows where ills resort:
they were bad times. None know what in his place
they might have done. I've my own faults to face.

Macquarie Place

I will go out and hear the strain
of rat-bag orators at large.
There is a battery in my brain
which just that fever might re-charge.

The blends of curious craziness
which crank and anarchist extol
could fill with their electric stress
the run-down fury of my soul.

Whether some economic scheme
to conquer currencies, and spread
over the honeyed earth its dream,
moves them, that all men may be fed;

or whether warnings of the worst
in drink or diet or the boss,
or judgement coming with a burst;
they bring back vision gone as loss.

For nudist, atheist, or pest,
half genius and half distraught,
has in his frenzy of unrest
the drive of some determining thought.

God keep me sane until my last
of breath or knowing; but let faint
fervour still reach me from the vast
madness of prophet and of saint.

I could proclaim the world is flat
with reasonable skill and wit,
but need fanatic zest if that
I would persuade myself of it.

So I will cross Macquarie Place
and covet zeal as crude as loud
in lunch-hour lunatics who face
amused indifference of the crowd.

J. A. R. McKELLAR

Love in a Cottage

(From "Fourth Napoleon")

Love in a cottage: candles in the dark
Of loneliness, a child to clasp the knee,
Three meals a day . . . O, undiscerning clerk,
Who ever voiced the wish to change with me. . . .

What can I show commensurate with his
Freedom in bondage? All his life is ruled
From this day till tomorrow until that
Falls on the Friday of his funeral.

Bread to be won, and, being won, be eaten;
Clothes to be bought, and being purchased, worn;
Children to get, and being got, be beaten;
Lips to be kissed, and being kissed, forsworn. . . .

Let him but look, and he can find direction,
And grumbling through his life he onward goes,
Convinced that he has not made the best selection
But satisfied as long as someone knows.

So will he stand him in a frozen trench,
Knee-deep in water, thimble-deep in rum,
Fighting Italians this year, next year French,
Content provided that his orders come,

Not caring much if God is on his side
Or if He shelters neutral in Monaco,
But swearing that his soul is crucified
If he be left without his own tobacco;

So will he perch him on an office stool
And cast up lines of figures into years

45

F

Content if someone checks his double rule
And buoys his heart with those mysterious fears

Of his employer's private conversation
Which the absorption of a little beer
Transmutes into a righteous indignation
Finding expression there but never here.

And so the least-born citizen of all
Goes onward with the firmness of the great,
Serene that should, by chance, the heavens fall
Someone will tell him how to put it straight. . . .

NORMA L. DAVIS

Daydreamers

The possum lies curled
In his high warm hut,
With his claws fur-furled
And his eyes fast shut;
While hawk-moths hide
In the spicy dark
On the underside
Of a gum's loose bark.
Bandicoots slumber
Deep in dry sags,
Sheathed in umber
Of old leaf rags.
Close in his cave
Beyond the gleams
Of the sun's gold lave,
The badger dreams
And snuffles and snores
With his nose in his paws.
The bittern lurks in a dusky clout
Of reeds on the edge
Of the marsh's sedge,

46

Waiting for night to lure him out.
While, mouse-fed and fat
And immaculate
As the homestead cat,
The mopoke clings to a curtained limb,
And cuddles his gnarled feet under him—
With his tufted ears
And his whiskered jowl
One almost fears
He is beast not owl.
Safe in his nest of twig and root
The wallaby-rat dreams rich red fruit
Lusciously swings from the wild sweet-briar,
And his soft nose twitches in sharp desire.
In rotting heaps
Of bracken wrack
The scorpion sleeps
With her poison sac;
While bats cling in holes
In dead tree-boles
Like little ripe pears of wintry brown
Waiting for dusk to shake them down.

LLYWELYN

Birds

(1)

Birds are our angels—out of heaven
And in our heaven, making it.
How can the soul expect to rise
That steals the rapture from the skies
To abnegate and prison it?

(2)

I would go forth and cry aloud
The *liberty* of lovely birds.

I would inscribe on every cloud
    That Love is god in rainbow words
But that my cries like theirs arise
    On callous earth and careless skies.

KEN BARRATT

Burke and Wills

I

So all men come at last to their Explorer's Tree,
Whereon they carve their valediction to the world.
Whether as they, we explore a continent, or are content
to explore ourselves, we find that mysterious centre,
that vast and utter loneliness, which is the heart of being;
we hear that silence more fatal than the siren's song.

II

Silence, like sound, has its eight note scale.
There is the silence after sound.
(After the farewell speeches, the well wishings,
the cheering as they rode proudly from Melbourne Town,
the silence of the bush.)
There is the silence of sound we cannot hear.
(The black men, always lurking, always watching,
never speaking, merging on the frieze of great untidy trees.)
There is the silence amid many voices.
(Often they spoke loudly, hoping to drive their fears away,
hoping to fill the empty air with assurance,
but the silence was in them.)
There is the silence of Death, of the voice that can never be
        heard again.
(After Grey died, he seemed to march with them still,
the invisible companion, not answering their questions,
not questioning their answers.)

There is the silence of Desolation.
(This was no Egypt, but cresting a sand dune,
they yet might discover the stones of a city, time devoured,
or glinting in the sun, a golden helmet, become a hive
for the patient labour of the bees.)
There is the silence of Despair.
(Returning to the depôt, finding it deserted,
they knew that words could buy them nothing
in this land of Nothing for Sale.)
There is the silence more ancient than man.
(Wills, the scientist, said it: *These rocks*
are so old, they have forgotten the singing
and the shouting of the sea, the violence
of the earth in the making.)
And last silence of all, completing the octave,
the silence that was before sound.
(Waiting for the end, life flowed backward to its source.
Voices, like a spring uncoiling,
receded and were superseded.
The last cry of hunger and pain
became the first cry for breath,
and now at last there was only the silence,
and they and the silence were one.)

III

Yet one man survived, one man returned
a little while to the world of men,
telling how Burke and Wills had died,
wresting the secret from a continent;
when they asked him to expound the secret,
he would speak of other things, saying rather,
"The camels gave us trouble from the beginning,"
or, *"Nardoo is no fit food for white men."*

A Volume of Chopin

Lady, I trust it is not to do harm
You bring that music here, under your arm;
And not to cause quick heat or sudden pallor
You've Indian autumn hair, that stooping colour
Of ripe maize. Moreover, ocean eyes
Which yet are not the sea, but the forget-
Me-not—which neither yet are flowers, but
To Chopin's buried soul, availing skies.

They do, these do, occasion me alarm.
Lady, I trust you come not to do harm.

The Lord in the Wind

Worship the Lord, the God of wild cold kind,
Water and wind,
Motionless trees,
And a change, and cries and silences.

The woods shake off a wild spray of old rain,
The stormy flowers are my very heart;
I worship thee again
Glory of strong trees, wet buds, and the sky!

I have laid a windy perfume on the stone;
Wood resin, and the blossom flame are nigh;
I have brought sweet wood, I come to dawn alone;
My prayer, keep grand the tempest in my heart!

The east is blenching now, and flames the stone;
My prayer, keep dew and anthem in my heart!

A. J. WOOD

From *Rolling John*

Rolling John and night together
Tumble down in stormy weather,
Rolling John and night together
Hi ho my bonny boy.

Where the jagged lightnings rend
Stormy skies from end to end
And the elements contend—
Hi ho my bonny boy.

So the midnight forests strain
And the world is wild with rain,
Rolling John comes out again
Hi ho my bonny boy.

. . . . . .

Taps at latches on the door
Thrice behind and thrice before,
What is it he searches for?
Hi ho my bonny boy.

Who he is we do not know,
Where he goes we cannot go,
We have never seen him so—
Hi ho my bonny boy.

. . . . . .

But when the branches plunge and rear
And air is piled on fiercest air
Rolling John's already there,
Hi ho my bonny boy.

Where the foam runs thick in trails
Of howling ships in howling gales
Rolling John is in the sails:
Hi ho my bonny boy.

Rolling John is in the chase
Where the rapid's waters race
To the weir's firm embrace:
Hi ho my bonny boy.

Where the desert's dreadful glare
Rarefies the rarest air
And fantastic forms appear—
Hi ho my bonny boy!

So the traveller, startled, sees
Upturned ships on upturned seas
In inverted sceneries . . .
Hi ho my bonny boy.

Where at early morning play
Things that only live a day
Flit about and fly away—
Hi ho my bonny boy—

Rolling John is in the air
Rolling John is everywhere,
Rolling John attend my prayer:
Hi ho my bonny boy!

A. D. HOPE

The Death of the Bird

For every bird there is this last migration:
Once more the cooling year kindles her heart;
With a warm passage to the summer station
Love pricks the course in lights across the chart.

Year after year a speck on the map, divided
By a whole hemisphere, summons her to come;
Season after season, sure and safely guided,
Going away she is also coming home.

And being home, memory becomes a passion
With which she feeds her brood and straws her nest
Aware of ghosts that haunt the heart's possession
And exiled love mourning within the breast.

The sands are green with a mirage of valleys;
The palm-tree casts a shadow not its own;
Down the long architrave of temple or palace
Blows a cool air from moorland scarps of stone.

And day by day the whisper of love grows stronger;
That delicate voice, more urgent with despair,
Custom and fear constraining her no longer,
Drives her at last on the waste leagues of air.

A vanishing speck in those inane dominions,
Single and frail, uncertain of her place,
Alone in the bright host of her companions,
Lost in the blue unfriendliness of space,

She feels it close now, the appointed season:
The invisible thread is broken as she flies;
Suddenly, without warning, without reason,
The guiding spark of instinct winks and dies.

Try as she will, the trackless world delivers
No way, the wilderness of light no sign,
The immense and complex map of hills and rivers
Mocks her small wisdom with its vast design.

And darkness rises from the eastern valleys,
And the winds buffet her with their hungry breath,
And the great earth, with neither grief nor malice,
Receives the tiny burden of her death.

Pyramis or The House of Ascent

This is their image: the desert and the wild,
A lone man digging, a nation piling stones
Under the lash in fear, in sweat, in haste;
Image of those demonic minds who build
To outlast time, spend life to house old bones—
This pyramid rising squarely in the waste!

I think of the great work, its secret lost;
The solid, blind, invincible masonry
Still challenges the heart. Neglect and greed
Have left it void and ruin; sun and frost
Fret it away; yet, all foretold, I see
The builder answering: "Let the work proceed!"

I think of how the work was hurried on:
Those terrible souls, the Pharaohs, those great Kings
Taking, like genius, their prerogative
Of blood, mind, treasure: "Tomorrow I shall be gone;
If you lack slaves, make war! The measure of things
Is man, and I of men. By this you live."

No act of time limits the procreant will
And to subdue men seems a little thing,
Seeing that in another world than this
The gods themselves unwilling await him still
And must be overcome; for thus the King
Takes, for all men, his apotheosis.

I think of other pyramids, not in stone,
The great, incredible monuments of art,
And of their builders, men who put aside
Consideration, dared, and stood alone,
Strengthening those powers that fence the failing heart:
Intemperate will and incorruptible pride.

The man alone digging his bones a hole;
The pyramid in the waste—whose images?
Blake's tower of vision defying the black air;
Milton twice blind groping about his soul
For exit, and Swift raving mad in his—
The builders of the pyramid everywhere!

An Epistle

EDWARD SACKVILLE TO VENETIA DIGBY

Ainsi, bruyante abeille, au retour du matin,
Je vois changer en miel les délices du thym.

First, last and always dearest, closest, best,
  Source of my travail and my rest,
The letter which I shall not send, I write
  To cheer my more than arctic night.
Sole day and all my summer in that year
  Of darkness, you were here,
Were here but yesterday, and still I go
  Rapt in its golden afterglow.
Caught in the webs of memory and desire,
  The cooling and the kindling fire,
Through all this house, from room to room I pace:
  Here at the stair we met; this place
You sat in; still I see you sitting there,
  As though some trace the printless air
Retained; a tremulous hush, as though you spoke,

55

Enchants its silence; here your cloak
I held for you and here you looked farewell
  And went, but did not break the spell,
By which I feel you here yet know you gone—
  So men, who winking see the sun
And turn into the dark, awhile descry
  His image on the dazzled eye.
But like a tale I tell it all again
  And gloss it with a scholar's pen,
For so Love, though he harvest all his store,
  Gleans in bare fields to make it more.
Now like the garner ant when frosts begin,
  I have my harvest heaped within:
Abundance for my year to come, a feast
  Still cherished, still increased;
For all it spends from its ripe yesterday
  The heart shall copiously repay:
Words, glances, motions, all that I rehearse
  My joy transfigures, as great verse
From music may have a perfection lent
  More than the poet knew or meant;
And as the cunning craftsman can prolong
  Through cadences and shifts of song,
And make what was by nature beautiful,
  By art more dulcet, keen and full,
So from one day, one meeting, I prepare
  Music to last me out the year.

Yet I cannot recall it as I should;
  Too much surprised by joy I stood,
A child who finds his long expected treat,
  Coming, too sudden and too sweet—
Or greedily I gulped it like a beast
  And missed the true, the lasting taste.

"Poor beast," I say, "poor beast, indeed, who comes
    To be content with scraps and crumbs!
Poor heart, poor Lazarus, overjoyed to wait
    The scrapings of another's plate!"
For, though I could restore, vivid and strong,
    That late, pure, breathless trance of song,
I know myself but a dumb listener, where
    I have sung bourdon to her air.

I that was rich, now at the treasury door
    May only glimpse that golden store
Piled in fantastic heaps; the jewelled shrine
    Worship, not touch, no longer mine;
At most, a starveling Tantalus, must see
    The shadow crop upon my tree
Slide through the hand and from my gaping lip
    The mocking naiad glide and slip.
Or rather—for in similes of woe
    I lose my way—full well I know
The food was real: 'Twas I who could not eat
    The spirit's insubstantial meat,
Pleasure of angels, such as flesh and blood
    Taste not, though all may take their food.
I, who have held you in my human arms,
    Must gaze as if on ghostly charms,
Or on the painting of a mistress dead—
    Yet we both breathe and might to bed.
To bed! At the mere thought I feel arise
    That rebel in the flesh, who cries:
"It was no picture we saw yesterday,
    But she, in all the living play
Of light on restless body, limbs, hair, breast,
    Eyes, hands—what need to tell the rest?"
What need? But, ah, what sure recourse of joy!
    This nothing can or shall destroy,

Custom deny nor honour stand between,
  Nor your own change of heart demean.
He whose you are, your husband and my friend
  —I do not grudge it, but commend—
Took, when he took you hence, your picture too
  Lest I should keep some part in you.
What should I care, who had my gallery lined,
  Crowded with pictures of the mind?
What care for silk or lutestring who possess
  The splendour of your nakedness,
The lily, the jet, the coral and the rose
  Varied in pleasure and repose?
Three years we lived as blessed angels do
  Who to each other show the true
Bareness of spirit and, only when they would
  Travel abroad, wear flesh and blood.
So clothed we met the world: at set of sun,
  Our foolish, needful business done,
Home we would turn, eager to taste at even
  Our native and our naked heaven.
So now by heart each single grace and all
  Their glowing postures I recall.
Absent, you come unbidden; present, you
  Walk naked to my naked view;
Dead, I could resurrect you from your dust;
  So exquisite, individual, just
The bare, bright flesh, I swear my eyes could tell
  You by throat, thighs or breast as well,
Or any least part almost, as your face.

  Alas, as courtiers out of place
Speak of the court, I boast and dream the rest.
  In exile now and dispossessed
I think of how we used, so long ago,
  In that tremendous overthrow

58

Of our first worlds, when first we loved, first knew
  No world except these selves, this Two,
How we would laugh to see that Last World pass
  For real beyond our Wall of Glass;
And we untouched, untouchable, serene,
  Plighted within our magic screen,
Would pity those without, whose curious eyes
  Could see, could judge, could recognize,
Know with the mind, but coldly and in part,
  Not with the comprehending heart.
This was our game; and, with the growth of love,
  We said, these walls of glass remove;
We re-embody those shadows by our joy;
  The frontiers of desire deploy
Until our latitudes of grace extend
  Round the great globe and bend
Back on themselves, to end where we begin
  Love's wars that take the whole world in.
So little states, rich in great men and sound
  In arts and virtues, gather ground
And grow to empires mighty in their day.
  And we, we said, more blest than they,
Shall not decline as Persian kingdoms do
  Or those the Tartar overthrew.
Who lives outside our universal state?
  And all within ourselves create.
Will angels fall twice, or the moon breed Turks?
  Or dread we our own works?—
But even while the architects designed
  The finials, their towers were mined.
He, your child-lover, twice reported dead,
  Once false—but all was false—some said
He died at Pont-de-Cé, and some said not
  But on rough alps his bones might rot—

For whom, though your heart grieved, it grieved as for
  Childhood itself that comes no more,
Yet came, and not as ghosts come from the grave,
  But as strong spirits come to save,
And claimed the love we buried long ago.
  I watched it rise and live. I know,
Alas, I know, though I believed it not,
  The spell he casts, who breaks the knot;
And this you told me once and bade me learn
  Even before his strange return.

Now it is I outside our Wall. I stand
  And once a year may kiss that hand
Which once with my whole body of man made free—
  Oh, my twice-lost Eurydice,
Twice must I make my journey down to Hell,
  Twice its grim gods by prayer compel,
And twice, to win you only for a day,
  The spirit's bitter reckoning pay,
Yet for my first default their just decree
  Grants me to hear you now and see,
As deserts know peace, as barren waters calms,
  Only forbidding me your arms.
Why, since my case is hopeless, do I still
  Exacerbate this wrench of will
Against the force of reason, honour, rest
  And all that is in manhood best?
Is not this second Orpheus worse than he
  Who perished in his misery,
Torn by the drunken women in their chase
  Among the echoing hills of Thrace?
To cherish and prolong the state I loathe
  Am I not drunk or mad or both?

Not so! These torments mind and heart approve,
    And are the sacrifice of love.
The soul sitting apart sees what I do,
    Who win powers more than Orpheus knew,
Though he tamed tigers and enchanted trees
    And broached the chthonic mysteries.
The gate beyond the gate that I found fast
    Has opened to your touch at last.
Nothing is lost for those who pass this door:
    They contemplate their world before
And in the carcass of the lion come
    Upon the unguessed honeycomb.
There are no words for this new happiness,
    But such as fables may express.
Fabling I tell it then as best I can:
    That pre-diluvian age of man
Most like had mighty poets, even as ours,
    Or grant them nobler themes and powers.
When Nature fashioned giants in the dew
    Surely the morning Muses too
Created genius in an ampler mould
    To celebrate her Age of Gold.
Yet think, for lack of letters all was lost,
    Think Homer's *Iliads* to our cost
Gone like those epics from before the Flood
    As, but for Cadmus, sure they would.

Books now preserve for us the boasts of time;
    But what preserved them in the Prime?
Where did they live, those royal poems then,
    But in the hearts and mouths of men,
Men of no special genius, talents, parts,
    Patience their sole gift, all their arts
Memory, the nurse, not mother, of ancient songs;
    No seraph from God's fire with tongs

G

Took the live coal and laid it on their lips;
  And yet, until their last eclipse,
Age after age, those giant harmonies
  Lodged in such brains, as birds in trees.
The music of the spheres, which no man's wit
  Conceives, once heard, he may transmit:
Love was that music, and by love indeed
  We serve the greater nature's need.
As on the rough back of some stream in flood
  Whose current is by rocks withstood,
We see in all that ruin and rush endure
  A form miraculously pure;
A standing wave through which the waters race
  Yet keeps its crystal shape and place,
So shapes and creatures of eternity
  We form or bear. Though more than we,
Their substance and their being we sustain
  Awhile, though they, not we, remain.
And, still, while we have part in them, we can
  Surpass the single reach of man,
Put on strange powers and vision we knew not of—
  And thus it has been with my love.
Fresh modes of being, unguessed forms of bliss
  Have been, are mine: But more than this,
Our bodies, aching in their blind embrace,
  Once thought they touched the pitch of grace.
Made for that end alone, in their delight,
  They thought that single act and rite
Paid nature's debt and heaven's. Even so
  There was a thing they could not know:

Nature, who makes each member to one end,
  May give it powers which transcend
Its first and fruitful purpose. When she made
  The Tongue for taste, who in the shade

Of summer vines, what speechless manlike brute,
  Biting sharp rind or sweeter fruit,
Could have conceived the improbable tale, the long
  Strange fable of the Speaking Tongue?
So Love, which Nature's craft at first designed
  For comfort and increase of kind,
Puts on another nature, grows to be
  The language of the mystery;
The heart resolves its chaos then, the soul
  Lucidly contemplates the whole
Just order of the random world; and through
  That dance she moves, and dances too.

JOHN THOMPSON

Letter to a Friend

Dear George,

  At last the blowfly's buzz retreats,
The sweats of summer fade, the autumn heats
Withdraw their torrid mantle. Winter comes.
No more the sharp mosquito whines and hums
Around the sleepers in their burning bed.
Keen winter nips them on the nose instead.
The sun, the regular soldier of the sky,
No longer flays us with his angry eye,
For mists and frosts and wild wet winds at last
Return—like friends recovered from the past.

One friend's away. What reason, what unreason,
Drives you to shun this retrospective season?
You should be here to pledge me drink for drink,
When, by my fire, into my chair I sink:
To bandy joke for joke, while stormy night
Rampages, rages, roars with all his might,
Whips the forsaken streets with whirling rains,

Rattles the doors, and shakes the window-panes.
You should be with me, while the claret flows,
Twisting and stroking your mustachios,
And mingling memories to revive the fun
Of all that we have seen and been and done.

Ah, George, a world of girls has learnt the trick
Since you and I first guttered at the wick;
A world of boys, ruled by unruly glands,
Swaggers and swells in ostentatious stands.
Let them. For us the ageing interchange
Of slack for tense, of ordinary for strange,
Offers the promise of approaching ease
Where actions fade to reminiscences.
Few have we known who tasted more than us
Folly's extremes or passion's overplus;
Few, too, who braved with such delightful strife
The incalculable cataract of life
To reach the central torrent, the clear sweep
Of confident waters channelling smooth and deep
Beyond all idle pools and foolish froth.
Thereby one truth is manifest to us both
(Not only for ourselves, for others too)
That each should do as he desires to do.

Inland and northward (would that you were here)
Nature walks with a blossom at each ear;
So, though my fire be snug, my cellar rich,
I cannot blame you for your restless itch.
Old though you be in every chromosome,
Go on, go further; for the more you roam
The finer fables you will bring back home.
Where are you drinking now, with rosy face?
In what unmapped or half-forgotten place

Plotting a detour of a thousand miles
To hunt for folk-songs or for crocodiles?
Upon what mangrove beach or coral cay
Animal-naked all the livelong day?
Above what mountain, borne on silver wings,
Flying your thirst to Broome or Alice Springs?

Mean minds, though they may cage the hawk or fox,
Cannot keep radium in a cardboard box;
They cannot strap up gales or gag the thunder
Or screw down clamps to hold an earthquake under;
Much less can they emasculate or kill
Man's giant affection, his titanic will,
Or the huge Joy that drives him up the cliffs
Of the most wild Perhapses and dangerous Ifs.
Dullness and Hatred, meeting no resistance,
Lose themselves in emptiness and distance,
But vital Gusto, bursting from duress,
Prospers in unrestraint and boundlessness.
Rejoice, dear George, in freedom. I admit
That, were you here, we'd talk with better wit
Of what we wish for than of what we did,
Long since, in bright Papeete or Madrid.
Above my roof the wrathy weather rolls;
Within, red orchids bloom among the coals.
Down the wet street belated taxis hiss;
Within, is warmth. Only yourself I miss.
Were I with you, how rousing it would be,
Over some murmuring moonlit tropic sea,
To steer for scenes unvisited before,
Cuzco, Mauritius, Bangkok, Travancore.
Enough, enough! Don't tempt me any more!
Loth as yourself the tether's length to learn,
I drink (from this full glass) to your return.

JOHN THOMPSON

The Adventurers

This is their third parting. Now she goes
Luminous-eyed and somewhat tragic, exalted
By such addition to her sum of action,
To tell her women friends. He promptly finds,
With his accustomed aptitude, fresh love—
Palm, lip, nipple, and satiny throat and reins
Sleek as a skinned rabbit's—and grins, and shrugs,
Copying forth the verses he keeps to hand
For new seductions under his great grapevine
Within his wall, where noon leopards the haunch
And the neat belly, puts light where hollows curve,
And sinks protuberances in limpid shadow.

Soon, encountering face to face in a café—
She with her curled hat-feather and eyelashes,
He with his ice-cold incandescent eye—
They nonchalantly speak of petty things,
The headlines and the weather, slightly hinting
A light disdain for either's romps and rorts
Now grown the sudden scandal of the city.
They bid Goodbye: then, two days later, meet
More privately, by accident. One week more,
They slap each other's cheeks in Martin Place,
And straightway their artesian passion jets
Anew. Oh never have there been such bores.

Now is the height and hurricane of their love.
Now do they beat and burn each other. Now
To all the world they telephone their jars
And jealousies, their stratagems and revenges.
Help, help! they cry. And rapidly, on the thrust
And thunderhead of the vehement commotion
Of their distraught advisers, pleaders, plotters,

And partisans, they feel themselves up-borne.
They swear that they will leap together, locked
And coupled, from a rooftop or a mountain;
May even marry; or may part forever;
Or must be false—they are, at once—to win
A mutual freedom; must resort to liquor—
They do, immediately—to defeat remorse.
Oh now they are most active, most alive,
Most glorified, most potent, and most happy,
Though suddenly neglectful of one another.

RONALD McCUAIG

Recitative

Waves rattling pebbles rocked me asleep,
But when I woke the waters were all still:
Dew on the wharf, and you—as tranquil
As in a dream; and only the swish and drip
Returning from my oars' returning sweep
Betrayed the silence and my schoolboy skill,
While the boat surged and slid, and the land fell
Into a line of shadows, dark and deep.

Then, when the sun broke red upon the lake
And burned its beams to roses in your hair,
I felt my hands tremble and my heart shake,
But you were all the morning, and you were
One with the dreaming water, still to wake,
Your kiss incurious as the windless air.

L'Après Midi d'une Fille aux Cheveux de Lin
(Homage to Debussy)

Bearing their birds and gardens on their hats
The ladies of suburbia have come,

Fresh in their sweeping skirts from sweeping mats,
To grace my mother's afternoon at-home.

For each, a delicately different china cup;
For all, the scandal and the price of eggs;
For me, my bright white sailor-suit starched up,
Its pinked seams chafing me between my legs,

And the white-frocked Renoir child with the flaxen hair
Tied in those chocolate-boxy bows he makes—
I am to take her to play in the open air,
Leaving her mother to the tea and cakes:

Into the stare of the afternoon sun at the grass
Wandering out in silence, hand in hand,
I, her diminutive and dutiful Pelleas,
She, my mysterious, miniature Melisande,

I see us yet, a portrait lost to tense,
Rapt in the heat as flowers in their aroma,
Fixed by the master's glaze of innocence. . . .
But life shakes rudely at pictorial coma:

The sweep has left behind his tin of soot—
These things must happen; why, I cannot tell:
For every Adam, his forbidden fruit,
For every Melisande, her destined well:

"Put in your head." The summer air is cursed
As Eden's with the scented breath of sin.
The fig-tree shudders. "You put yours in first."
The bamboo stirs and sighs. My head goes in.

My sailor-suit, the glow of Renoir's paint,
Become our weekly charwoman's despair,

Life's evil critic, throwing off restraint,
Empties his inkpot on the flaxen hair.

    Golliwogs, now, we
    Run in to show the
        People what we have done.
We cause a creaking of the tight-laced sitters.
    Somebody shrieking,
    Everyone speaking,
        One of them drops her bun.
They all seek hiding-places for their titters.

And we are trapped in passion's aftermath,
The prophecy and prototype of others—
The double expiation of the bath,
The hissings of the geyser and the mothers,

Conclude this formal afternoon at-home.
I wonder would she think me past all shame,
Rejoicing in the roses of her small, spanked bottom,
A lover of Renoirs who has forgotten her name?

Au Tombeau de Mon Père

I went on Friday afternoons
Among the knives and forks and spoons
Where mounted grindstones flanked the floor
To my father's office door.

So serious a man was he,
The Buyer for the Cutlery. . . .
I found him sketching lamps from stock
In his big stock-records book,

And when he turned the page to me:
"Not bad for an old codger, eh?"
I thought this frivolous in him,
Preferring what he said to them:

They wanted reparations paid
In German gold and not in trade,
But he rebuked such attitudes:
"You'll have to take it out in goods."

And what they did in time was just,
He said, what he had said they must:
If Time had any end in sight
It was, to prove my father right.

The evening came, and changed him coats,
Produced a rag and rubbed his boots,
And then a mirror and a brush
And smoothed his beard and his moustache;

A sign for blinds outside to fall
On shelves and showcases, and all
Their hammers, chisels, planes and spades,
And pocket-knives with seven blades.

Then, in the lift, the patted back:
"He's growing like you, Mr Mac!"
(The hearty voices thus implied
A reason for our mutual pride.)

And so the front-door roundabout
Gathered us in and swept us out
To sausage, tea in separate pots,
And jellies crowned with creamy clots.

And once he took me on to a
Recital, to hear Seidel play,
And Hutchens spanked the piano-bass,
Never looking where it was.

When I got home I practised this,
But somehow always seemed to miss,
And my cigar-box violin,
After Seidel's, sounded thin.

And once he took me to a bill
Of sporadic vaudeville.
A man and woman held the stage;
She sneered in simulated rage,

And when he made a shrewd reply
He'd lift his oval shirt-front high
And slap his bare and hairy chest
To celebrate his raucous jest.

Then, as the shout of joy ensued,
Uniting mime and multitude,
And mine rang out an octave higher,
A boy-soprano's in that choir,

My father's smile was half unease,
Half pleasure in his power to please:
"Try not to laugh so loudly, Ron;
Those women think you're catching on."

But far more often it was to
The School of Arts we used to go;
Up the dusty stairway's gloom,
Through the musty reading-room

And out to a veranda-seat
Overlooking Hunter Street.
There in the dark my father sat,
Pipe in mouth, to meditate.

A cake-shop glowed across the way
With a rainbow-cake display;
I never saw its keeper there,
And never saw a customer,

And yet there was activity
High in the south-western sky:
A bottle flashing on a sign
Advertising someone's wine.

So, as my father thought and thought
—Considering lines of saws he'd bought,
Or, silence both his church and club,
Feeling close to Nature's hub,

Or maybe merely practising
Never saying anything,
Since he could go, when deeply stirred,
Months, at home, without a word,

Or pondering the indignity
Of having to put up with me—
I contemplated, half awake,
The flashing wine, the glowing cake:

The wine that no one can decant,
And the cake we didn't want:
As Mr Blake's Redeemer said,
"This the wine, and this the bread."

ERIC IRVIN

Christmas 1942
(New Guinea)

I

Here's shade and comfort by this towering tree,
Dear Phaedrus, and a breeze to lull our rest.
Here let our thoughts flow undisturbed and free
As flows Laloki. Many sands have run
Since by Ilissus you and I reclined;
And many comrades journeyed to the sun
With whom we have shared everything but death.

II

I could not speak of them on my return;
I could not bare the wound so closely wrapped
Against corruption by the spoken word;
My smile the dreamer's shield held up to guard
A sense of impotence, a deep despair
Of making "over here" see "over there".

But someone spoke of Damas and Djezzine,
And phrased a pretty speech about Tobruk,
And in a flash the cramped suburban room,
The silly teacups and the linen cloth,
The heartless sympathy of common speech
Moved out beyond the compass of Time's reach:

And I was in a man's world, and the earth
Shook or stood still as we chose to dictate;
And life was ours, and death, and the sweet pain
Of thinking now and then of other days
When we were human beings, sheltered, fed;
The darlings of existence, fancy-led.

73

III

Bitterness sways me but a while: is gone,
And I remember mornings such as this
By such a green-banked, slowly-flowing stream
An aeon of experience ago.
Remember, too, a love that down the years
Has mocked me with its echoed might-have-been.

These notes I gather now; all chords resolve
In pointed harmony phrased by despair;
New-cadenced by regrets that rise and fall;
That hint a solemn pity: and are gone.

EVE LANGLEY

Native Born

In a white gully among fungus red
Where serpent logs lay hissing at the air,
I found a kangaroo. Tall, dewy, dead,
So like a woman, she lay silent there,
Her ivory hands, black-nailed, crossed on her breast,
Her skin of sun and moon hues, fallen cold.
Her brown eyes lay like rivers come to rest
And death had made her black mouth harsh and old.
Beside her in the ashes I sat deep
And mourned for her, but had no native song
To flatter death, while down the ploughlands steep
Dark young Camelli whistled loud and long,
"Love, liberty and Italy are all."
Broad golden was his breast against the sun.
I saw his wattle whip rise high and fall
Across the slim mare's flanks, and one by one
She drew the furrows after her as he
Flapped like a gull behind her, climbing high,

74

Chanting his oaths and lashing soundingly,
While from the mare came once a blowing sigh.
The dew upon the kangaroo's white side
Had melted. Time was whirling high around,
Like the thin woomera, and from heaven wide
He, the bull-roarer, made continuous sound.
Incarnate, lay my country by my hand:
Her long hot days, bushfires and speaking rains,
Her mornings of opal and the copper band
Of smoke around the sunlight on the plains.
Globed in fire bodies the meat-ants ran
To taste her flesh and linked us as we lay,
For ever Australian, listening to a man
From careless Italy, swearing at our day.
When, golden-lipped, the eagle-hawks came down
Hissing and whistling to eat of lovely her,
And the blowflies with their shields of purple brown
Plied hatching to and fro across her fur,
I burnt her with the logs, and stood all day
Among the ashes, pressing home the flame
Till woman, logs and dreams were scorched away,
And native with night, that land from where they came.

ELIZABETH RIDDELL

Wakeful in the Township

Barks the melancholy dog,
Swims in the stream the shadowy fish.
Who would live in a country town
If they had their wish?

When the sun comes hurrying up
I will take the circus train
That cries, cries once in the night
And then not again.

In the stream the shadowy fish
Sleeps below the sleeping fly.
Many around me straitly sleep
But not I.

Near my window a drowsy bird
Flickers its feathers against the thorn.
Around the township's single light
My people die and are born.

I will join the circus train
For mangy leopard and tinsel girl
And the trotting horses' great white haunches
Whiter than a pearl.

When to the dark blue mountains
My captive pigeons flew
I'd no heart to lure them back
With wheat upon the dew.

When the dog at morning
Whines upon the frost
I shall be in another place,
Lost, lost, lost.

Under the Casuarina

The garrulous old man who once had owned
An island in a pale and fronded sea
(All ships dropped anchor there, all sailormen
Climbed past his coco-palms to drink with him
And eat his goat steaks and his mermaid soup)
Lies dreaming under the casuarina-tree,
His pink old mouth gone back to childhood pout,
His washed old eyes as vacant and as blue

As his new-born great-grandson's, his old rump
Shrunken and sagged in a chair, his tired old legs stretched
   out . . .

The dotard and the baby so are met. But where's the boy
Who chased the lightning, where the youth who lied
And kissed and fought and squandered, where the man
Who married a woman for her wild red hair
And under her lash of tongue and temper lived
And bore with her in hatred till she died?

"A Frenchman named the island—all red soil
Papaws and pineapple and spotted gum,
Pandanus and the oleander blowing
White petals everywhere, but not a drop
Of water in her. Then the long drought came.
That was the end of growing."

Somewhere there went the child, the youth, the man,
Gone with sea eagles down the windy sky,
Off with the sailors and away to sea,
Buried in the red soil under pandanus roots,
A sharpener for cat's claws.
What's left sleeps in a chair, and when it can
Babbles to strangers, such as you and I.

R. D. MURPHY

Back Lane

A ribald and unbuttoned air
Plays about on all things there:
Confidentially, the sly
Palings lean to the passer-by,
Where prancing in the wind are seen

77

The elements of Mrs Green.
Opinions and underclothes are aired
In chalk, on clotheslines—secrets shared,
While he may easily read, who jogs,
The running commentary of dogs.
In a vacant lot paspalum breeds
With dock and nut-grass, a slum of weeds;
In this neglected spot are laid
Memorials to the sly-grog trade;
Night's haunted by the ghosts of fish
And bursts of feline gibberish:
And on this compost, like a rose,
Fragrance of children's laughter blows.

ROBERT CLARK

Generations

My mother's form was spare and keen:
Soft hills there are with shadows between.

My father's creed was tense and fierce:
Dark pools invite and the rain drops pierce.

I learned of God between four walls:
He dwells where plover to lover calls.

My brain was washed with heaven's light:
The world's an apple for teeth to bite.

We paced the floor of one small room:
A child inscribed its walls with doom.

Their way was Right, all else was Wrong:
A carefree girl took me along.

And yet, I am the plough-share blade
That, from their steel, life's forge has made,

And by my side two children stand
Waiting their turn to work the land.

MARY FINNIN

The Farm Near Norman's Lane

That old man at the farm near Norman's Lane,
(Wormwood and horehound winding all the way)—
Waits for his sons to change,
For times to come again
To the hard row
His father had to hoe.

(Show them what's what, he thinks,
The old man marking time at the wicket gate;
And best of all, not worry him a bit,
Snug sandwiched in life's troubles
Like bread about salt meat.)

Niggard as noonday shade,
He stands at the wicket gate—
A break in the gorse hedge flowing
Over its lurking shadow.

"Times are too good; but still 'n all
Them terriers have the mange,
(They catch it from the foxes on the hill);
Kero and mutton fat's the stuff;
I'll mix it soon;
Soon as ye've gone.
But wait in the sun.

"A man in armour now—
You'd fix him with a drop of oil at the joints;
But my old woman stiffens in her bed;
And medicine don't do a mite of good."

He has dressed the soil to rape it over again.
His features, carved to petulance, endure.
His nose divides the wind, his eyes
Smoulder in caves of darkness,
As he fronts the sea beyond his boundaries.
Far more
Than the skylarks to show for his sixty years:

A scratch-bright car; all fences strained and strong;
And three spoilt sons to brawl with all day long;
That girl too smart for her own good, wanting the best;
Wife wading through pain to an isle of painless rest.

But skylarks poise, like Simeon Stylites;
Standing on air, they sing
Of capeweed spread for one long, yellow day.
Tomorrow will beat up an easterly swell,
Flood the sea marsh, salt down another spring.

W. HART-SMITH

A Sequence from "Christopher Columbus"

I. CIPANGU

Elbows in wine-slops, news of the ocean isles
they tell in taverns under a stinking lamp.

Madre de Dios, here is evidence!

And once a swollen corpse, a woman's,
naked, tattooed, face-down in a scum
of jellyfish and weed. . . .

And bits of wood to Santo sometimes come,
most strangely carved.

The woman drowned, they say, had almond eyes.
Masters, a ship, a ship, for my youth dies!

2. DEPARTURE

Being at last on our way,
a great calmness came upon my soul,
as if all creation waited on my will.
I was at that moment made whole.

A forest of masts in the bay,
and seeming to grow from the buildings of the city;
a square sail there with a golden cross
wrinkling in the sun. But O the pity,

that I should find this dark procession of Jews
winding out of our country; and their wailing
in my ears this day of sailing.

3. SPACE

Columbus looks towards the New World,
the sea is flat and nothing breaks the rim
of the world's disc;
he takes the sphere with him.

Day into night the same, the only change
the living variation at the core

of this man's universe;
and silent on the silver ship he broods.

Red gouts of weed, and skimming fish, to crack
the stupefying emptiness of sea;
night, and the unimpassioned gaze of stars. . . .

And God be praised for the compass, oaths
bawled in the fo'c'sle,
broken heads and wine,
song and guitars,

the tramp of boots,
the wash and whip of brine.

4. COMES FOG AND MIST

. . . and all the sails hang limp.

The ship is the core of a pearl;
we are enclosed.

Lord God, the mist; there is no need of it
here on your ocean sea, for we
are already lost.

It has its own
mysterious sound, and you call
the softest murmur of a girl's
lips speech, then this is all

one continuous whisper whispering. . . .

Here fine gold hair upon my wrist
grows pearls.

Lord God, the mist,
and we, already lost.

5. THE WATERSPOUT

Forward lay sunlight silver on the sea;
behind, the darkness of a cavern;
from it a wind, and cloud-arms over the wind
towards the ship.

They saw a rope of cloud twist down
and a tongue of sea drawn up as the whirlwind blew,
drinking the ocean up in a plume of foam.
"Santa Maria, look! . . . how far is home!"

And some knelt down, some checked their blasphemy,
eyes wide and mouths wide, dumb.
Columbus watching, touched his brow and breast.
"Christ be with us!" he said, as the ship sped west.

IAN MUDIE

They'll Tell You About Me

Me, I'm the man that dug the Murray for Sturt to sail down,
I am the one that rode beside the man from Snowy River,
and I'm Ned Kelly's surviving brother (or did I marry his
    sister?
I forgot which), and it was my thumbnail that wrote that
    Clancy
had gone a-droving, and when wood was scarce I set the grass
    on fire
and ran with it three miles to boil my billy, only to find
I'd left the tea and sugar back with my tucker-bag.
And it was me, and only me, that shot through with the
    padre's daughter,

83

shot through with her on the original Bondi tram.
But it's a lie that I died hanging from a parrot's nest
with my arm in the hollow limb when my horse moved
    from under me;
I never die, I'm like the Leichhardt survivor I discovered
fifty years after the party had disappeared, I never die.
I'm Lasseter and Leichhardt both, I joined the wires of the
    O.T.
so that Todd could send the first message from Adelaide to
    Darwin;
I settled everywhere long before the explorers arrived,
my tracks criss-cross the Simpson Desert like city streets,
and I've hung my hat on Poeppel's Peg a thousand times.
It was me who boiled my billy under the coolabah,
told the bloke in the flash car to open his own flamin' gates,
put the goldfields pipeline through where the experts said
    nobody could,
wanted to know "Who's robbing this coach, you or Ned
    Kelly?"
left the dog guarding my tucker-box outside of Gundagai,
yarned with Tom Collins while we fished for a cod some-
    one'd caught years before,
and gave Henry Lawson the plots to make his stories from.
Me, I found a hundred wrecked galleons on the Queensland
    coast
dripping with doubloons, moidores, and golden Inca swords,
and dug a dozen piles of guelders from a Westralian beach;
I was the one that invented the hollow woodheap,
and I built the Transcontinental, despite heat, dust, death,
    thirst, and flies.
I led the ragged thirteen, I fought at Eureka and Gallipoli
    and Lae,
and I was a day too early (or was it too late?) to discover
    Coolgardie,
lost my original Broken Hill share in a hand of cribbage,

had the old man kangaroo pinch my coat and wallet,
threw fifty heads in a row in the big game at Kal,
took a paddle-steamer seventy miles out of the Darling on a
    heavy dew,
then tamed a Gippsland bunyip and sooled him on
to capture the Tantanoola Tiger and Fisher's Ghost
and became Billy Hughes's secretary for a couple of weeks.
Me, I outshore Jacky Howe, gave Buckley his chance,
seem to remember riding a white bull through the streets of
    Wagga,
and have had more lonely drinks than Jimmy Woods:
I jumped across Govett's Leap and wore an overcoat in
    Marble Bar,
sailed a cutter down the Kindur to the Inland Sea,
and never travelled till I went to Moonta.
Me, I was the first man ever to climb to the top of Ayers Rock,
pinched one of the Devil's Marbles for the kids to play with,
drained the mud from the Yarra, sold the Coathanger for a
    gold brick,
and asked for beer off the ice at Innamincka.

Me—yesterday I was rumour,
today I am legend,
tomorrow, history.
If you'd like to know more of me
inquire at the pub at Tennant Creek
or at any drover's camp
or shearing-shed
or shout any bloke in any bar a drink
or yarn to any bloke asleep on any beach,
they'll tell you about me,
they'll tell you more than I know myself.
After all, they were the ones that created me,
even though I'm bigger than any of them now
—in fact, I'm all of them rolled into one.

For anyone to kill me he'd have to kill
every single Australian,
every single one of them,
every single one.

Wilderness Theme

I saw that country in a dream
—its empty earth, its searing breath,
its burning stones, its stars—the land
some know as life and some as death.

I trudged across unending plains
(hero or midget, which was I?)
while from above stared down at me
a vastness of unwinking sky.

I did not heed the dried-up creeks,
I did not feel the blowing sand,
but, like Sturt's pattering sheep, my days
gained strength from what seemed barren ground

I seek again that scene in dreams
—the blazing stars, the ochre earth,
the stones, the shining flowers—the land
some see as life and some as death.

Dingoes shall race to gnaw my bones,
the roaring winds unearth my skull;
say only this—that all my days
with that persistent search were full.

Waratah

In the time when swan and swan
down the grey half light were gone,
through fire-blackened scrub he came
where, in resurrected flame,
the waratah rose from its steep
above the organ-sounding deep.
There, in that rock-bare region made
cold by rain, he stood and prayed
that the poet's coal of pain
burn and brand his brow again.
In the time when swan and swan
with their creaking cries were gone,
sudden, all the ashened west
burst and seared his face and breast.
Round him rock and scrub on fire
stood out fused in one desire,
where the fierce flower from its steep
flamed upon the sounding deep.

The Lyre-bird

Hushed to inaudible sound the deepening rain
closed round me on those ridges where the road
had led me to hunger and darkness, and again
I heard its voice on leaves. I eased my load
against a rock and found the tea-tree flowering
out of the dark wet bush, and drew its spray
of close-starred blossom over me with showering
of cold rain on my face. And when my way
led down through rocks, the lyre-bird halted me
with those full rich repeated notes that sprang
out of the darkness and the sound of rain, and he

was silent then but, as I waited, sang
again. Past roots and trees I went along
rich with that flowering, rich with repeated song.

The Tank

Where once the grey scrub's finches cried with thin
voices through the heat their *"nin-nin-nin,"*
bursts now the golden burgeon of this change
before the gibber-plain, the pale blue range.
Here to the fettlers' sunken water tank
the blacks came in; their three dun camels sank
down to their knees; the tall and bearded blacks
unslung the water-drums tied to the packs,
filled them, and called their camels and were gone
to where, out on the iron plain, led on
their lubras, children and lean dogs . . . to know
always the ranges' distant ebb and flow,
the wind-whorled sands that bare the parched white bone,
beneath their feet, the knife-sharp gibber-stone.

Rock-lily

The rock-lily's pale spray,
like sunlight, halts my way
up through the unpierced hush
of birdless blue-grey bush.
The rocks crouch on their knees
in earth, torsos of trees
and limb-boughs lead up where
the cliff-face scales the air.
Out from you, rock, my friend,
I lean and, reaching, bend
the scentless pale spray back
to me and see the black

spots in each orchid flower.
O, my love, what power
keeps you curled and bound?
Tormented, the earth's round
begins again. What rock
holds you where you lock
yourself from me? Alone
this spray breaks from the stone.

JOHN BLIGHT

Becalmed

Above and below the ship, this blue:
No cloud, no island, and which of two
Suns was celestial, submarine?
Each sailor shrugged. Who'd ever been
South of the Line . . . who knew . . . who knew?

There was a vessel in the sky—
Towering above, or below the eye?
If only something would drift past,
Seaweed or cloud to foul its mast.
Why should it, too, becalmed thus, lie?

Below and above, the seeming sea
Like a great eye which dreamily
Sees nothing, and by nothing is seen;
A waking that may, may not, have been.
"Which of us now is you, is me?"

Everything double under the sun;
And doubly doubled to prove which one
Is under which, which sun above.
"God, if the counterpart would move."
But movement there or here is none.

"Silver's a man is full of cunning;
Monkey, he is on the taffrail running;
Agile, he props and dives right in.
One rises to meet him with a grin.
Head strikes head with a smack that's stunning.

"No more Silver, he's under the sea;
Or up in the sky, or where is he?"
Lost in the ether, south of the Line;
The eight bells rang, but we heard nine:
And where are we, and where are we?

Lord, it is dark. The two suns met
In a blaze of flame we won't forget:
And which ate which, we could not say;
But night came on and at close of day
We cheered. "All's not proved double yet."

Too soon, too soon! The moon that rose
Split into two, like silver shoes:
One walked the sky, one walked the sea;
But which walked which was strange to me:
For south of the Line, who knows . . . who knows?

"This is the other half," I said.
"Since Egypt, here they've buried the dead,
Under the earth and south of the Line."
The eight bells rang and we heard nine.
"We are they whom the mermaids wed."

Doomed on a ship that is dead, becalmed;
In a winding sheet of blue, embalmed.
"Friend, it is doubly strange I feel,
No one will credit our plight was real;
We dead, in a ship that is dead, becalmed."

JOHN BLIGHT

Death of a Whale

When the mouse died, there was a sort of pity:
The tiny, delicate creature made for grief.
Yesterday, instead, the dead whale on the reef
Drew an excited multitude to the jetty.
How must a whale die to wring a tear?
Lugubrious death of a whale; the big
Feast for the gulls and sharks; the tug
Of the tide simulating life still there,
Until the air, polluted, swings this way
Like a door ajar from a slaughterhouse.
Pooh! pooh! spare us, give us the death of a mouse
By its tiny hole; not this in our lovely bay.
—Sorry, we are, too, when a child dies;
But at the immolation of a race, who cries?

FLEXMORE HUDSON

Mallee in October

When clear October suns unfold
mallee tips of red and gold,

children on their way to school
discover tadpoles in a pool,

iceplants sheathed in beaded glass,
spider orchids and shivery grass,

webs with globes of dew alight,
budgerigars on their first flight,

tottery lambs and a stilty foal,
a papery slough that a snake shed whole,

and a bronzewing's nest of twigs so few
that both the sky and the eggs show through.

91

The Golden Bird

I watched the new moon fly
behind a summit tree
to perch on an upper branch
and so look down at me.

Upon that very instant,
the glowing gully rang
with a kookaburra's laughter,
while frogs and crickets sang.

I was a dreamy lad,
walking the bush alone:
it was thirty years ago. . . .
In all that I have known,

the frogs have never croaked,
the crickets never chirred,
so blithely as on that night
when the moon was a laughing bird,

new moon, a golden bird,
perched high, with beak in air,
when I was a dreamy lad
and the bush was everywhere.

Ship from Thames

Stay, ship from Thames, with fettered sails
in Sydney Cove this ebb of tide;
your gear untangled from the gales,
imprisoned at your anchor ride.

The portly gentlemen, who are
the pillars of the land, come down

and greet the Newcomes voyaged far
to make a name in Sydney Town.

The redcoats, too, with shouldered arms,
marshal pale wretches from the hold,
who, cramped in tempests and in calms,
have learned to do as they are told.

Flash phaetons fill the streets to-day;
inn-tables rock to sailor fists;
the Governor, while the town is gay,
checks over new assignment lists.

Aloof, the slandered and abhorred
behold from off a quarried rise
the cause of all the stir abroad,
a fiercer glitter in their eyes.

KENNETH MACKENZIE

Heat

"Well, this is where I go down to the river,"
the traveller with me said, and turned aside
out of the burnt road, through the black trees
spiking the slope, and went down, and never
came back into the heat from water's ease
in which he swooned, in cool joy, and died.

Often since then, in brutal days of summer
I have remembered him, with envy too;
thought of him sinking down above his knees
in a cold torrent, senseless of the rumour
of death gone down behind him through the trees,
through the dead grass and bushes he shoved through.

93

I

He must have tasted water after walking
miles and miles along that stream of road,
gulping and drooling it out of his mouth
that had for one day been too dry for talking
as we went on through drought into the south
shouldering leaden heat for double load.

Plainly he couldn't bear it any longer.
Like the hand of a bored devil placed
mercilessly upon a man's head,
it maddened him. I was a little stronger
and knew the river, rich with many dead,
lustrous and very cold, but two-faced

like some cold, vigorous, enticing woman
quite at the mercy of her remote source
and past springs. I could not warn him now—
not if he were here now. I could warn no man
while these red winds and summer lightnings blow
frantic with heat across my dogged course

into the south, beside the narrow river
which has that traveller's flesh and bones, and more.
Often I see him walking down that slope
thirsty and mad, never to return, never
quenched quite of his thirst, or of his hope
that heat would be arrested on its shore.

A Fairy Tale

(For Elisabeth)

Why should you wake, my darling, at this hour,
in this unhaunted nurse-room of your sleep?
The street is silent, echoing your screams
with shocked politeness; the clock ticks past four—
it is no time for dreams.

Only a vanishing trail of footsteps keeps
smartly in time with time. Come—turn over,
hide your twisted face under the blue cover,
and cover your bared soul with shaking hands:
It is too naked, and we are alone,
and I am not young enough to understand,
only to pity your trembling stare,
your hopeless moaning.
Terror has struck me, too; it is older than age,
old as the simple cell, old as air,
helplessly aware of doom—
the last page turning—
but why in the fastidious silence of this room?

Am I to believe, in spite of night,
sleep, solitude, security, warmth, love
all nursing you, your mind, remembering,
heard the sound of engines in flight?
Through the dark skin of sleep did come
the roar of the drumskin, and the whistling?
The drum—did you hear the drum?
Maybe then, with the whole world turned to metal
you watched through shut eyes on the eyelids' screen
the abattoirs in action, much death
of howling flesh, but not the flesh of cattle.
Between the taking and the relinquishment of a breath
all that will be, is, must have been,
backwards and forwards on the screen runs
in chaos, generating terror, griping
the tangle of bowels—the fighting on the dunes,
slaughter among mountains, under suns
torrid and dusty, in snows, in the dark,
in the dawn and at twilight. Death sniping
merrily from the void wipes out a city,
and with a mighty shout as of one voice

we all scream "Pity—give pity! And money!" and then
are seen, in the exploding crash and roar
of chambered flame released, to be men
(or women) impressed by so much devastation:
The like of it has never been seen before,
and it's the proof of our age, civilization.
You see it in a bombshell in the night,
and you, my darling, suck it out of the air
into your sleep, and dream it really is true.
No! this is a fairy story for small girls,
a tale so well-devised, so rare,
it even convinced you!
Wait till to-morrow's imperial dawn unfolds
its east red-white-blue banner, you will see
nothing so evil under such a flag could be.

Turn and sleep again.
The sound you dreamed was just our old friend thunder
roaring with pain.
The wet and splashing torrents, that showed red
through eyelids closed on open dreaming eyes,
were only rain,
and the footsteps have walked up into the sky,
away at the street's end. In this bed
is nothing but a small warm girl who must
always, always sleep very peacefully
and not scream in the night—

                                        (I trust. I trust.)

Table-birds

The match-bark of the younger dog sets fire to
an indignation of turkeys under the olives.
Scurf-wigged like senescent judges, drum-puffing desire,
they bloat their wattles, and the chorus gives

a purple biased judgment on the pup:
Trouble enough, pup, bloody trouble enough!

So much for morning and the sun's generous
flattery of the metal of their feathers.
Noon makes them somnolent, dusty, glad to drowse
the fly-slurred hours of midday August weather
in scooped hollows under the ripe trees
whose fruit sweetens them for the Christmas season.

The tilted sun, the craw's shrunk emptiness
wake them to stir their lice and strut again,
head back, tail spread, and dangling crest
and greedy, angered eye. . . . The spinsterly hen
blinks the lewd fan and frets among the grains,
knife-grey and sleek, hungrier, less restrained

by stifling turkey pride beneath the red
slap of the leering comb. But they submit.
The fan snaps to; head doubles over head—
and day's escape delineates them fitfully
like darkness clotted into nervous shapes
under the olives, in whose night they sleep.

An Old Inmate

Joe Green Joe Green O how are you doing today?
I'm well, he said, and the bones of his head looked noble.
That night they wheeled Joe Green on a whisper away
but his voice rang on in the ward: I'm a terrible trouble
to all you girls. I make you work for your pay.
If I 'ad my way I'd see that they paid you double.

Joe Green Joe Green for eighty-two years and more
you walked the earth of your granddad's farm down-river

where oranges bigger than suns grow back from the shore
in the dark straight groves. Your love of life was a fever
that polished your eye and glowed in your cheek the more
the more you aged and pulsed in your voice for ever.

Joe Green looked down on his worked-out hands with scorn
and tears of age and sickness and pride and wonder
lay on his yellow cheek where the grooves were worn
shallow and straight: but the scorn of his look was tender
like a lover's who hears reproaches meet to be borne
and his voice no more than echoed its outdoor thunder;

Gi' me the good old days and the old-time folk.
You don't find that sort now you clever young fellers.
Wireless, motorbikes all this American talk
and the pitchers and atom-bombs. O' course it follers
soon you'll forget 'ow to read or think or walk—
and there won't be one o' you sleeps at night on your pillers!

Joe Green Joe Green let us hear what your granddad said
when you were a lad and the oranges not yet planted
on the deep soil where the dark wild children played,
the land that Governor King himself had granted
fifteen decades ago that the Green men made
a mile-square Eden where nothing that lived there wanted.

Joe Green lay back and smiled at the western sun:
"Fear God and the women, boy," was his only lesson,
"and love 'em—but on the 'ole just leave 'em alone,
the women specially." Maybe I didn't listen
all of the time. A man ain't made of stone. . . .
But I done my share of praying and fearing and kissing.

No. I 'ad no dad nor mum of me own—
not to remember—but still I'd a good upbringing.

98

The gran'ma raised thirty-two of us all alone
child and grandchild. . . . Somewhere a bell goes ringing.
Steps and the shielded lanterns come and are gone.
The old voice rocks with laughter and tears and singing.

Gi' me the good old days. . . . Joe Green Joe Green
how are you doing tonight? Is it cold work dying?
Not 'alf so cold as some of the frosts I've seen
out Sackville way. . . . The voice holds fast defying
sleep and silence, the whisper and the trifold screen
and the futile difficult sounds of his old girl's crying.

Legerdemain

Ah me the hand upon the body
    the whorled speech
that sings from fingertips a wordless melody
      mounting with the delicate increasing touch
      to a long cry in the mind can never reach
      the end of the search.

Night has a thousand I O U's
    signed with sighs
shaken out of the blood that floods imperious
      the flesh touched delicately and by day these
      flutter unhonoured along habitual byways
      past averted eyes.

Or perhaps one that said *tomorrow*
    is redeemed
by accident on the stair or in the mirror
      where eyes look curiously into eyes doomed
      for ever to look back curiously or dimmed
      by what they dreamed.

For not eyes but hands only can see
    in night's alley
that leads from nowhere nowhere and keeps busy
    the shuddering direction-finder love's ally
    pointing a staggering track to melancholy
    through heaven's valley.

Ah me the seeing skin reports
    certain replies
signalling a hasty offering of transports
    and through the dark viaduct the eyeless music plays
    with drums diminishing and frantic pleas
    keep moving please.

The hand upon the body dies instead
    of reason dying
though for some moments consciousness insisted
    reason had died in the divine undoing
    of ties with earth.
                Sense now steadying
    hears spirit crying.

Pat Young

(For Pat, 7. 9. 48)

The composition of Pat Young
—Glory be and my! oh my!—
is a fine bone and fire along it
—Glory my!

Over the bone the nervous mesh
—Glory my!—
springs out into the vivid flesh
—Glory be and my!

And on the lively flesh the skin
—Glory be and my! oh my!—
lets the touch of fingers in
—Heavens above!

The fingers' touch, the laugh, the look
—Glory gracious!—
lay her page open like a book
—Glory be!

And all the nerve, and all the bone
—Heavens bless us!—
are yet not Pat Young alone
—Glory!

For she is sweetly sour and fresh
—God forgive us!—
as fruit that makes the dew more precious
—Gracious!

And all along the hollow bone
—Bless my soul!—
Patricia lives her life alone
—Glory be and my! oh my!

Also, within the nervy net
—God defend us!—
she nurses up a wicked wit
—Christmas!

The wit defends the nerves; the nerves
—Glory be and my! Glory!—
defend the dream. The dream serves
—Forgive me, Lord!—

as god and honesty and love
—Heavens! Heavens!—
which all her composition proves
—Glory be!

DOUGLAS STEWART

The Snow-gum

It is the snow-gum silently,
In noon's blue and the silvery
Flowering of light on snow,
Performing its slow miracle
Where upon drift and icicle
Perfect lies its shadow.

Leaf upon leaf's fidelity,
The creamy trunk's solidity,
The full-grown curve of the crown,
It is the tree's perfection
Now shown in clear reflection
Like flakes of soft grey stone.

Out of the granite's eternity,
Out of the winters' long enmity,
Something is done on the snow;
And the silver light like ecstasy
Flows where the green tree perfectly
Curves to its perfect shadow.

Mahony's Mountain

If there's a fox, he said, I'll whistle the beggar;
And shrill the counterfeit cry of the rabbit's pain
Rang out in the misty clearing; so soon to be lost
In the stony spurs and candlebarks darker and huger

Where Mahony's mountain towers in drifts of rain.
No sharp wild face out of burrow or hollow stump,
No rustle shaking the raindrops from rushes or flowers
—Greenhood and bulbine lily lighting the swamp—
Nothing but bush and silence; so on and up
Tramping through moss where so many violets cluster
You cannot help but crush them; and still more steep
The sheep-track winds through the dripping leaves and the
    rocks,
And still no fox, no bandicoot's tiny fluster,
No flurry of green rosellas flashing past,
Nothing but the huge grey silence, the trees and—look,
There where the mountain breaks on its granite peak,
The doubletail orchid, O like some fairytale fox,
Whistled from earth by a wilder call than ours,
Pricks up its yellow ears and stares through the mist.

Brindabella

Once on a silver and green day, rich to remember,
When thick over sky and gully rolled winter's grey wave
And one lost magpie was straying on Brindabella
I heard the mountain talking in a tall green cave
Between the pillars of the trees and the moss below:
It made no sound but talked to itself in snow.

All the white words were falling through the timber
Down from the old grey thought to the flesh of rock
And some were of silence and patience, and spring after
    winter,
Tidings for leaves to catch and roots to soak,
And most were of being the earth and floating in space
Alone with its weather through all the time there is.

Then it was, struck with wonder at this soliloquy,
The magpie lifting his beak by the frozen fern
Sent out one ray of a carol, softened and silvery,
Strange through the trees as sunlight's pale return,
Then cocked his black head and listened, hunched from the
    cold,
Watching that white whisper fill his green world.

The Silkworms

All their lives in a box! What generations,
What centuries of masters, not meaning to be cruel
But needing their labour, taught these creatures such patience
That now though sunlight strikes on the eye's dark jewel
Or moonlight breathes on the wing they do not stir
But like the ghosts of moths crouch silent there.

Look, it's a child's toy! There is no lid even,
They can climb, they can fly, and the whole world's their
    tree;
But hush, they say in themselves, we are in prison.
There is no word to tell them that they are free,
And they are not; ancestral voices bind them
In dream too deep for wind or word to find them.

Even in the young, each like a little dragon
Ramping and green upon his mulberry leaf,
So full of life, it seems, the voice has spoken:
They hide where there is food, where they are safe,
And the voice whispers, "Spin the cocoon,
Sleep, sleep, you shall be wrapped in me soon."

Now is their hour, when they wake from that long swoon;
Their pale curved wings are marked in a pattern of leaves,
Shadowy for trees, white for the dance of the moon;

And when on summer nights the buddleia gives
Its nectar like lilac wine for insects mating
They drink its fragrance and shiver, impatient with waiting,

They stir, they think they will go. Then they remember
It was forbidden, forbidden, ever to go out;
The Hands are on guard outside like claps of thunder,
The ancestral voice says Don't, and they do not.
Still the night calls them to unimaginable bliss
But there is terror around them, the vast, the abyss,

And here is the tribe that they know, in their known place,
They are gentle and kind together, they are safe for ever,
And all shall be answered at last when they embrace.
White moth moves closer to moth, lover to lover.
There is that pang of joy on the edge of dying—
Their soft wings whirr, they dream that they are flying.

Nesting Time

Oh never in this hard world was such an absurd
Charming utterly disarming little bird,
The mossy green, the sunlit honey-eater
That darts from scribbly-gum to banksia-tree
And lights upon the head of my small daughter.

It must decide, for men and birds alike,
As pick-pick-pick it goes with its sharp beak,
If so much trust is possible in Nature;
And back it darts to that safe banksia-tree
Then swoops on my own head, the brave wild creature.

It thinks it must have hair to line its nest
And hair will have, and it will chance the rest;
And up and down my neck and then my daughter's

Those prickly black feet run, that tugging beak,
And loud like wind it whirrs its green wing-feathers.

Then take your choice from me or those fair tresses
You darting bird too shy for our caresses;
There's just this gap in Nature and in man
Where birds can perch on heads and pull out hair
And if you want to chance it, well, you can.

The Garden of Ships

Even so deep in the jungle they were not safe.
The stars still glittered round them like barbed wire
But more than that, fantastic below the cliff
A lantern filled a tree with orange fire
Like a great tropical flower, one window's gleam
With a round yellow eye stared up at them.

If it was another village of the dog-faced people
As seemed most likely, no one ran out to bark;
And the tree seemed bare and tapering, more like a steeple
Where the light like a golden bell rocked in the dark.
Was it the mast of a ship?—impossibly lost
Here in the forest, mile upon mile from the coast?

They could climb down and creep on it through the jungle
For lights meant men, and men meant water and food
And they were thirsty enough, and they were hungry;
But when had the lights of men ever brought them good?
Not in these evil islands, not in these times;
But years ago, it seemed, in the country of dreams.

All night long they talked about it in whispers.
They would have liked to sleep, for they had come far
By burning and naked seas, by sliding rivers,

By islands smouldering still with the smoke of war
Or shrouded in steam, to reach this ridge at last;
But how could they sleep with that strange light on the mast?

And sometimes water glimmered, sometimes it seemed
That ranging away from the lantern, tree by tree
Or mast by mast, whole fleets of vessels gleamed
Faint in the starshine where no ships could be.
And in the morning they were ships indeed!
It was amazing, Marco Polo said,

Speaking of his own travels to that island,
How such a current surged there through the ocean
It seized upon wandering ships and dragged them inland;
And leaping against the hills in white explosion
Tore by their roots the tall trees out of the jungle;
And up the long gulf, in one vast helpless tangle,

Swept them along, tall ships and trees together,
And drove more timber in and piled it up
So they lay locked at the end of the gulf for ever
While many a merchant mourned his missing ship.
But what was more amazing, though for that matter
Likely enough to happen with trees and water,

Was how while the ships lay still as they did now
High-decked, tall-masted, flotsam from all the seas,
Junks from old China, sampan, Arabian dhow,
Galleon and barque, Dutch, English, Portuguese,
Their anchors green with moss, their sails all furled,
Never again to ride the waves of the world,

That wall of trees, as silt filled up the shallows,
Took root again and stood up tall and green
And taller grew and flung their leafy shadows

From ship to ship with flowering vines between,
Hanging the masts with such enchanting burden
It seemed the fleet was anchored in a garden.

And there were gardeners too—that was the thing,
Piercingly strange, that moved the watchers most;
Far down, unseen, they heard a woman sing,
She might have been a bird there, or a ghost;
But windows opened, plumes of smoke rose up,
Brown men in sarongs walked about each ship

And all the jungle rang with children's laughter;
And they saw too, not least of many solaces,
Where bridges joined the ships across the water,
Bare-breasted girls who walked among the trellises
Or white and golden, fair as waterlilies,
Plunged in the pools and swam with gleaming bodies.

So, ragged and bony, wild-eyed with war and fever,
They came down out of the jungle to the clearing
And truly they thought they could lie down there for ever,
Feasting on fruit, drinking the palm-wine, hearing
The laughter and the music, the lap of the tide
Stealing so far from the sea to the ship's side,

And those soft voices telling the old stories
Of how they had lived on the ships for generations,
And if the dog-faced people on their forays
Chanced on their haven, people of all the nations
Living in peace together untouched by the world,
They lifted up their dog-faced heads and howled

And fled, thinking them spirits. So too, long after
When the war and all their journeying turned to a dream,
Like a wild vision they had seen in their fever,

Even to these two wanderers did they seem;
For calling them always with its clear compulsion
Somewhere over the mountains, across the ocean,

With its broad golden fields, its urgent cities,
Its ports where ships still sailed on whatever venture,
Their homeland lay; and though like waterlilies
The fair girls swam and the birds sang in rapture
And the old ships dreamed in the jungle; even so,
Now they were strong they could reach it, and they must go.

A. G. AUSTIN

Chez-Nous
(Tobruk)

In my cave lives a solitary rat,
(A celibate rat,
I can vouch for that);
He hasn't a mate for miles around
And he lives on what he can find on the ground,
Though the country's such
That that's not much.
I don't like he
And he can't stand me
But we need the roof so there we be.

In my cave lives a type of flea,
(A scurrilous flea
Believe you me);
And though he's such a tiny thing
His bite is worse than a scorpion's sting.
He lives on Rat,
But worse than that
He lives on me

K

This scurrilous flea
With all his numerous progeny.

Near my cave lives the octave bird,
(The queerest bird
You've ever heard);
He sings eight notes as he climbs the scale
Though the topmost note is known to fail.
He's very small,
Just like us all.
So in we fit
Though we're cramped a bit—
Old Rat
And Flea
And Bird
And Me.

MAURICE BIGGS

Spring Offensive, 1941

In where the smoke runs black against the snow,
And bullets drum against the rocks, he went,
And saw men die, with childish wonderment—
Where bayonets glitter in the sudden glow,
And sleek shells scream, and mortars cough below:
There tanks lurch up, and shudder to a halt
Before the superb anger of the guns:
Then flares go up—the rattle of a bolt—
Rifles stutter—and voices curse the Huns. . . .
And then, he jerked and toppled to the ground,
His ears too full of noise, his eyes of light;
His scattered cartridge clips glint brassy-bright;
A Vickers cackles madly from a mound. . . .

Oh, where the red anemone brims over
To swarm in brambled riot down a rise,
There we will lay him, lay your widow'd lover,
And wipe the poor burnt face, and gently cover
The look of startled wonder in the eyes. . . .
Let Beauty come, let her alone
Bemoan those broken lips with kisses from her own.

Greece, April 1941

DAVID CAMPBELL

Harry Pearce

I sat beside the red stock route
And chewed a blade of bitter grass
And saw in mirage on the plain
A bullock wagon pass.
Old Harry Pearce was with his team.
"The flies are bad," I said to him.

The leaders felt his whip. It did
Me good to hear old Harry swear,
And in the heat of noon it seemed
His bullocks walked on air.
Suspended in the amber sky
They hauled the wool to Gundagai.

He walked in Time across the plain,
An old man walking in the air,
For years he wandered in my brain;
And now he lodges here.
And he may drive his cattle still
When Time with us has had his will.

Men in Green

Oh, there were fifteen men in green,
Each with a tommy-gun,
Who leapt into my plane at dawn;
We rose to meet the sun.

We set our course towards the east
And climbed into the day
Till the ribbed jungle underneath
Like a giant fossil lay.

We climbed towards the distant range
Where two white paws of cloud
Clutched at the shoulders of the pass;
The green men laughed aloud.

They did not fear the ape-like cloud
That climbed the mountain crest
And hung from twisted ropes of air
With thunder in their breast.

They did not fear the summer's sun
In whose hot centre lie
A hundred hissing cannon shells
For the unwatchful eye.

And when on Dobadura's field
We landed, each man raised
His thumb towards the open sky;
But to their right I gazed.

For fifteen men in jungle green
Rose from the kunai grass
And came towards the plane. My men

In silence watched them pass;
It seemed they looked upon themselves
In Time's prophetic glass.

Oh, there were some leaned on a stick
And some on stretchers lay,
But few walked on their own two feet
In the early green of day.

They had not feared the ape-like cloud
That climbed the mountain crest;
They had not feared the summer's sun
With bullets for their breast.

Their eyes were bright, their looks were dull,
Their skin had turned to clay.
Nature had met them in the night
And stalked them in the day.

And I think still of men in green
On the Soputa track
With fifteen spitting tommy-guns
To keep a jungle back.

Night Sowing

O gentle, gentle land
Where the green ear shall grow,
Now you are edged with light:
The moon has crisped the fallow,
The furrows run with night.

This is the season's hour:
While couples are in bed,
I sow the paddocks late,
Scatter like sparks the seed
And see the dark ignite.

O gentle land, I sow
The heart's living grain.
Stars draw their harrows over,
Dews send their melting rain:
I meet you as a lover.

Ariel

Frost and snow, frost and snow:
The old ram scratches with a frozen toe
At silver tussocks in the payable mist
And stuffs his belly like a treasure chest.

His tracks run green up the mountainside
Where he throws a shadow like a storm-cloud's hide;
He has tossed the sun in a fire of thorns,
And a little bird whistles between his horns.

"Sweet-pretty-creature!" sings the matchstick bird,
And on height and in chasm his voice is heard;
Like a bell of ice or the crack of the frost
It rings in the ears of his grazing host.

"Sweet-pretty-creature!" While all is as still
As the bird on the ram on the frozen hill,
O the wagtail warms to his tiny art
And glaciers move through the great beast's heart.

Pallid Cuckoo

Alone the pallid cuckoo now
Fills his clear bottles in the dew:
Four five six seven—climb with him!
And eight brings morning to the brim.

Then from green hills in single file
My ewes and lambs come down the scale:
Four three two one—the matrons pass
And fill their bellies up with grass.

But in the evening light the lambs
Forget their hillward-munching dams;
To cuckoo pipes their dances start
And fill and overflow the heart.

JOHN MANIFOLD

The Bunyip and the Whistling Kettle

I knew a most superior camper
  Whose methods were absurdly wrong;
He did not live on tea and damper
  But took a little stove along.

And every place he came to settle
  He spread with gadgets saving toil;
He even had a whistling kettle
  To warn him it was on the boil.

Beneath the waratahs and wattles,
  Boronia and coolabah,
He scattered paper, cans, and bottles,
  And parked his nasty little car.

He camped, this sacrilegious stranger
  (The moon was at the full that week),
Once in a spot that teemed with danger
  Beside a bunyip-haunted creek.

He spread his junk but did not plunder,
  Hoping to stay the week-end long;

He watched the bloodshot sun go under
Across the silent billabong.

He ate canned food without demurring,
He put the kettle on for tea.
He did not see the water stirring
Far out beside a sunken tree.

Then, for the day had made him swelter
And night was hot and tense to spring,
He donned a bathing suit in shelter
And left the firelight's friendly ring.

He felt the water kiss and tingle.
He heard the silence—none too soon!
A ripple broke against the shingle,
And dark with blood it met the moon.

Abandoned in the hush, the kettle
Screamed as it guessed its master's plight,
And loud it screamed, the lifeless metal,
Far into the malicious night.

The Tomb of Lt. John Learmonth, A.I.F.

"At the end on Crete he took to the hills, and said he'd fight it out with only a revolver. He was a great soldier." . . .

—*One of his men in a letter.*

This is not sorrow, this is work: I build
A cairn of words over a silent man,
My friend John Learmonth whom the Germans killed.

There was no word of hero in his plan;
Verse should have been his love and peace his trade,
But history turned him to a partisan.

Far from the battle as his bones are laid
Crete will remember him. Remember well,
Mountains of Crete, the Second Field Brigade!

Say Crete, and there is little more to tell
Of muddle tall as treachery, despair
And black defeat resounding like a bell;

But bring the magnifying focus near
And in contempt of muddle and defeat
The old heroic virtues still appear.

Australian blood where hot and icy meet
(James Hogg and Lermontov were of his kin)
Lie still and fertilize the fields of Crete.

* * *

Schoolboy, I watched his ballading begin:
Billy and bullocky and billabong,
Our properties of childhood, all were in.

I heard the air though not the undersong,
The fierceness and resolve; but all the same
They're the tradition, and tradition's strong.

Swagman and bushranger die hard, die game,
Die fighting, like that wild colonial boy—
Jack Dowling, says the ballad, was his name.

He also spun his pistol like a toy,
Turned to the hills like wolf or kangaroo,
And faced destruction with a bitter joy.

His freedom gave him nothing else to do
But set his back against his family tree
And fight the better for the fact he knew

He was as good as dead. Because the sea
Was closed and the air dark and the land lost,
"They'll never capture me alive," said he.

*   *   *

That's courage chemically pure, uncrossed
With sacrifice or duty or career,
Which counts and pays in ready coin the cost

Of holding course. Armies are not its sphere
Where all's contrived to achieve its counterfeit;
It swears with discipline, it's volunteer.

I could as hardly make a moral fit
Around it as around a lightning flash.
There is no moral, that's the point of it,

No moral, but I'm glad of this panache
That sparkles, as from flint, from us and steel,
True to no crown nor presidential sash

Nor flag nor fame. Let others mourn and feel
He died for nothing: nothings have their place.
While thus the kind and civilized conceal

This spring of unsuspected inward grace
And look on death as equals, I am filled
With queer affection for the human race.

Gordon Childe

From this far, late-come country that still keeps
A primitive and ancient dream, he drew
That which is name- and changeless. Here he grew
And, all his work accomplished, here he sleeps.

Scholar and man, his road lay straight through time.
With rational affection he restored
From shards the tool by which the race explored
Its world and heaven, risen from the slime

Not on the wings of mystery but through shared
Dread and experience. Ranging free, he saw
The gods, with Caesar one before the law
Of birth and death, decay—and God not spared.

Our prehistoric father who was sent
To his last journey with an axe of stone,
With this same axe cut through the dark unknown
The road on which Saul to Damascus went.

And so, come home, he closed the book and cast
Upon the fertile wind his unwrit page.
Dying, the hills stood round him, age on age,
Man makes himself. Each crest out-tops the last.

MICHAEL THWAITES

Thermopylae

The story, as now we see, was over-written
By Herodotus, bless his warm Hellenic heart!
Emotion swayed him—the drama of his theme,
The cosmic battle-canvas, East and West,

Darkness and light, Barbarian versus Greek,
Free men conjoined to hurl the tyrant back
And rescue civilization. Who can blame
The artist's eye for kindling on such matter?
A case, what's more, if not beyond dispute
At least compelling, when you contemplate
That surge of genius startling and sublime
That, like a spring from some unfathomed sea,
Rose in the wake of Persia's routed horde.

And so he drew it larger than the life
In black and white, abjuring shades of grey,
Dwelt hard on Xerxes' barbarous fits of rage,
His impious, dark, un-Greek activities,
Nor scrupled, where it helped his picture out,
To rearrange the date of an eclipse
Or (patriot wish being father to the thought)
To multiply by ten the Persian forces
Deployed against the Greek so-splendid few
Whose valour needed no extravagance.

Therefore he stands convicted in his tracks,
Father of History, by conclusive tests
Found wanting, biased, partial, and involved,
By zeal misled, and quick credulity.
This we concede, and honour justly those
Who sift the fact with fierce integrity.
We have come a journey, can no more return
Where lofty Truth may over-ride what's true,
Great faith excuse small falsehood. Here we stand
Exiles for ever from that treacherous ground.

But can we come again to that great heart
And that large spirit capable of fire?
We who live habitually in the Hot Gates

Between the precipitous mountains and the sea,
Dulled with the din of conflict, shall we find
The Spartan wholeness in our world's most need?
How shall we grasp how momently we are choosing
Ourselves to be that vast obsequious army
Hurried on the ebb and flow of tyrant tides,
Or those three hundred named and nameless men
Who died in the pass, and will not die again?

JUDITH WRIGHT

The Bull

In the olive darkness of the sally-trees
silently moved the air from night to day.
The summer-grass was thick with honey-daisies
where he, a curled god, a red Jupiter,
heavy with power among his women lay.

But summer's bubble-sound of sweet creek-water
dwindles and is silent; the seeding grasses
grow harsh, and wind and frost in the black sallies
roughen the sleek-haired slopes. Seek him out, then,
the angry god betrayed, whose godhead passes,

and down the hillsides drive him from his mob.
What enemy steals his strength—what rival steals
his mastered cows? His thunders powerless,
the red storm of his body shrunk with fear,
runs the great bull, the dogs upon his heels.

The Twins

Not because of their beauty—though they are slender
as saplings of white cedar, and long as lilies—
not because of their delicate dancing step

or their brown hair sideways blown like the manes of fillies—
it is not for their beauty that the crowd in the street
wavers like dry leaves around them on the wind.
It is the chord, the intricate unison
of one and one, strikes home to the watcher's mind.

How sweet is the double gesture, the mirror-answer;
same hand woven in same, like arm in arm.
Salt blood like tears freshens the crowd's dry veins,
and moving in its web of time and harm
the unloved heart asks, "Where is my reply,
my kin, my answer? I am driven and alone."
Their serene eyes seek nothing. They walk by.
They move into the future and are gone.

Wonga Vine

Look down; be still.
The sunburst day's on fire,
O twilight bell,
flower of the wonga vine.

I gather you
out of his withering light.
Sleep there, red;
sleep there, yellow and white.

Move as the creek
moves to its hidden pool.
The sun has eyes of fire;
be my white waterfall.

Lie on my eyes like hands,
let no sun shine—
O twilight bell,
flower of the wonga vine.

The Hawthorn Hedge

How long ago she planted the hawthorn hedge—
she forgets how long ago—
that barrier thorn across the hungry ridge;
thorn and snow.

It is twice as tall as the rider on the tall mare
who draws his reins to peer
in through the bee-hung blossom. Let him stare.
No one is here.

Only the mad old girl from the hut on the hill,
unkempt as an old tree.
She will hide away if you wave your hand or call;
she will not see.

Year-long, wind turns her grindstone heart and whets
a thornbranch like a knife,
shouting in winter "Death"; and when the white bud sets,
more loudly, "Life."

She has forgotten when she planted the hawthorn hedge;
that thorn, that green, that snow;
birdsong and sun dazzled across the ridge—
it was long ago.

Her hands were strong in the earth, her glance on the sky,
her song was sweet on the wind.
The hawthorn hedge took root, grew wild and high
to hide behind.

Bullocky

Beside his heavy-shouldered team,
thirsty with drought and chilled with rain,
he weathered all the striding years
till they ran widdershins in his brain:

Till the long solitary tracks
etched deeper with each lurching load
were populous before his eyes,
and fiends and angels used his road.

All the long straining journey grew
a mad apocalyptic dream,
and he old Moses, and the slaves
his suffering and stubborn team.

Then in his evening camp beneath
the half-light pillars of the trees
he filled the steepled cone of night
with shouted prayers and prophecies.

While past the camp fire's crimson ring
the star-struck darkness cupped him round,
and centuries of cattlebells
rang with their sweet uneasy sound.

Grass is across the waggon-tracks,
and plough strikes bone beneath the grass,
and vineyards cover all the slopes
where the dead teams were used to pass.

O vine, grow close upon that bone
and hold it with your rooted hand.
The prophet Moses feeds the grape,
and fruitful is the Promised Land.

South of My Days

South of my days' circle, part of my blood's country,
rises that tableland, high delicate outline
of bony slopes wincing under the winter,
low trees blue-leaved and olive, outcropping granite—

clean, lean, hungry country. The creek's leaf-silenced,
willow-choked, the slope a tangle of medlar and crab-apple
branching over and under, blotched with a green lichen;
and the old cottage lurches in for shelter.

O cold the black-frost night. The walls draw in to the
    warmth
and the old roof cracks its joints; the slung kettle
hisses a leak on the fire. Hardly to be believed that summer
will turn up again some day in a wave of rambler roses,
thrust its hot face in here to tell another yarn—
a story old Dan can spin into a blanket against the winter.
Seventy years of stories he clutches round his bones.
Seventy summers are hived in him like old honey.

Droving that year, Charleville to the Hunter,
nineteen-one it was, and the drought beginning;
sixty head left at the McIntyre, the mud round them
hardened like iron; and the yellow boy died
in the sulky ahead with the gear, but the horse went on,
stopped at the Sandy Camp and waited in the evening.
It was the flies we seen first, swarming like bees.
Came to the Hunter, three hundred head of a thousand—
cruel to keep them alive—and the river was dust.

Or mustering up in the Bogongs in the autumn
when the blizzards came early. Brought them down; we
    brought them
down, what aren't there yet. Or driving for Cobb's on the
    run
up from Tamworth—Thunderbolt at the top of Hungry Hill,
and I give him a wink. I wouldn't wait long, Fred,
not if I was you; the troopers are just behind,
coming for that job at the Hillgrove. He went like a luny,
him on his big black horse.

Oh, they slide and they vanish
as he shuffles the years like a pack of conjurors' cards.
True or not, it's all the same; and the frost on the roof
cracks like a whip, and the back-log breaks into ash.
Wake, old man. This is winter, and the yarns are over.
No one is listening.
    South of my days' circle
I know it dark against the stars, the high lean country
full of old stories that still go walking in my sleep.

The Old Prison

The rows of cells are unroofed,
a flute for the wind's mouth,
who comes with a breath of ice
from the blue caves of the south.

O dark and fierce day:
the wind like an angry bee
hunts for the black honey
in the pits of the hollow sea.

Waves of shadow wash
the empty shell bone-bare,
and like a bone it sings
a bitter song of air.

Who built and laboured here?
The wind and the sea say
—Their cold nest is broken
and they are blown away.

They did not breed nor love.
Each in his cell alone
cried as the wind now cries
through this flute of stone.

Woman to Man

The eyeless labourer in the night,
the selfless, shapeless seed I hold,
builds for its resurrection day—
silent and swift and deep from sight
foresees the unimagined light.

This is no child with a child's face;
this has no name to name it by:
yet you and I have known it well.
This is our hunter and our chase,
the third who lay in our embrace.

This is the strength that your arm knows,
the arc of flesh that is my breast,
the precise crystals of our eyes.
This is the blood's wild tree that grows
the intricate and folded rose.

This is the maker and the made;
this is the question and reply;
the blind head butting at the dark,
the blaze of light along the blade.
Oh hold me, for I am afraid.

Storm

On the headland's grassed and sheltered side,
out of the wind I crouch and watch
while driven by the seaward ship-destroying storm
races of insane processional breakers come.
A long-dead divine authority reflows the tide
at evening, and already the gnawed hill of beach
alters and shrinks. The waves cry out: Let us be done.

Let us be done with the long submission, the whips—
that hurl us for ever on time's frigid stone
mouthing our ever-repeated plea for an answer and getting
    none.
Let us break free, smash down the land's gate
and drown all questions under a black flood.
Hate, then, the waves cry: hate.

And round each headland of the world, each drenching rock,
crowding each wild spray-drop, as in the womb's calm lying,
they beat and whirl on the waves, the invisible legion
of momentary crystals, less-than-a-second's-tick
lives, love's first and everywhere creation;
so small, so strong, that nothing of all this mad rock-torn
surge and violence, not the storm's final desperation
touches them,
busy in the unhurt stillness, breeding and dying.

MARGARET IRVIN

Chanticleer

Chanticleer makes canticles
To rumour in the night;
And from his spurs, along his wings
Runs the metal of his praise—
Though silver and the sheen are one,
The russet and the rust are met
In the dark thickets under dawn
Where his prophetic voice is set.

The dreamer in his narrow dream
Hears, far off, his treason told,
That took him to the edge of death
Which tempted him with ceaseless sleep,
And shielded him, as once the womb.

Chanticleer cries his alarm
Which, thrice-repeated, is a hymn:
The struggle and the sun foretold,
And that, from each impassive dream,
Repentantly the sleepers come.

HAROLD STEWART

Lament in Autumn

Wu Tao-tzŭ (alone):

"The year and I are dying out together:
The cold, the damp, descend on all our weather.
The long warm afternoons that would extend
So late into the west there seemed no end
To those the abundant summer had in store,
Have long outworn the golden tone they wore—
Their ample warmth returns in me no more;
Too late now in our enervated day
To argue fruitlessly against decay,
When fading leaves have interspersed with sere
The head of verdure on the ageing year.
Though with much twisting it, I should prepare
A long long rope out of my whitening hair,
Oh, still it would not fathom my despair!
This green and yellow ache without relief,
This numb internal bruise will not be brief:
Its melancholic present, evergreen;
Its yellow past, eaten by might-have-been.
Congealing in the core of bone and bole,
The once-impulsive sap slows, and the soul
With branches bare, hints at the shed leaf
Of nameless discontent, which is my grief.
O weary leaf in exile, are you now
As homesick, as my heart is, for the bough?

And do you miss, as I, familiar leaves?
And is this rain falls down and wets my sleeves?
Sorrow corrodes the heart that disbelieves.
My days turn sallow too, touched by the stain
Of tears. My tree stands rusting in the rain.
The dead leaf drops; the dying leaves remain;
Till those few left to me break off at last,
And melting in the mould of autumns past,
Leave no remembered skeleton of veins,
But in the chronic anguish merge their pains.
In these dejected woods the exhausted year
And I still linger; but it darkens here:
The skies grow overcast with rain, and drear.
So, with the first large drops at random starting,
Our lagging hour advances for departing.
Summer already dead, our day is set;
But still we cling, and still regret, regret. . . ."

The Leaf-makers

There was an ancient craftsman once, who made
A silken-green semitransparent jade
To imitate a living mulberry leaf.
Minutely carved and delicate in relief,
Its map of veins and lucid arteries
Seemed to flow with the cool green blood of trees.
Three years of patient handicraft, intent
Upon this leaf-like portrait, had he spent
So that intricate cutting could indent
Around its profile every nick and notch,
And even turn to a rain-discoloured blotch
Russet with which the mineral was laced,
So perfectly was imperfection placed.
Before the Prince of Sung he then displayed,
Polished to glossiness, the finished jade;

And when the lapidary's work was laid
Among fresh mulberry leaves to rival them,
A silkworm, curious with hunger, picked
The leaf of artifice: its senses tricked,
It tried to bite the jade from tip to stem!
The Prince of Sung unwittingly allowed
Wonder to change his face, and so endowed
The artisan with patronage and praise
For skill that could outwit an insect's gaze.
Hearing of which, Lieh-tzŭ countered: "Now,
If it should take as long as that for Tao
To make a single bud unfold with care
Its crinkled wing into the spring's harsh air,
Seldom would trees have anything to wear!"

VAL VALLIS

Fishing Season

Old Fisherwoman:
The wave that is dark piles white and slips to its death.
The dorsal grey whirls in the shining break
Of fins in flight, red-stippled, stayed and slain.
The black net wades ashore, straddling its paunch
And spews its silver gorgings on the sand.
Now, in the time of barrenness on earth
Has come our season of rejoicing. Strong
The wind-wolves bayed beyond the rising moon.
We heard their crying on the autumnal gusts
Sou'west of summer; saw their frost-dark feet
Trample to mud the late green of the season.
The hedge-waves whiten with swifter flowers than spring;
And feeding salmon rocket from the sea.

131

Young Fisherwoman:
Call back the men who have gone to cast their nets.
The white of the gull beyond the harbour bar
Dipped to the boil of the waters. Call them back!
For the gull's wing low smears white at the face of the cliff
And the grey of the gull has stained the racing clouds.
Like a blood-shot eye in the gaping skull of the wind
The red flag burns on the mast at the harbour office,
And in night's eye the pupil of the moon
Dilates in its iris of cloud-barren space.
These are not times for men to dare the sea,
When moon and wind and water plot against them.

Old Fisherwoman:
Be still, young wife. Giant mackerel sweep the coast,
And Dorey tells of salmon near the Rip.
Soon will the mackerel pass, and salmon move
Up Townsville way, and what will summer bring
But gathering shells and time for beaching hulls?
Hear this from one who lost her son at sea.
I stood upon the pier and watched his sail
Shake out its wings, and on his deck there fell
The shadow and I saw him in its darkness.
The churning porpoise rolled before his bows;
The aimless turtle rose. The curlew cried
The note of all the sorrow of the world.
They tell me, who were in the dinghy with him,
He chanced upon the loosened yarn of night
And from the unravelling skies was hauling in
A thread of tangled stars, when the sea leapt up
To draw him down with arms as cold as death
And wrap him in the meshes I had made.
The green wave, in the autumn of his blood,
At sunrise drifted brown about the shore.
Hold down your fear, and drown it in your heart.

Young Fisherwoman:
How can I still the mounting gale in me?
Death is the only answer that fulfils
Each question-mark the wind-curled waves imply.

Old Fisherwoman:
I say the salmon and the mackerel leap
Off-shore. Though finning death may scourge the shoals,
They flood, a living tide, about our coast. . . .
And this, when sewing up the hole he'd made
I held the torn mesh to the lamp that night
And through its tasselled cave a face met mine.
Death grinned at me, like a spider from its web,
Thieving his glances from the flickering lamp.
The flame burned low, depleted by his theft,
And aimlessly my fingers plied the needle.
When, at sunrise, night and tears grown old,
I saw the harbour waking through the mesh,
Death was my prisoner. The net was whole again;
Its knotted squares of toil had walled him in,
And only promises of spangled scales
Silvered its patterned air. There was no room
For him to shelter in my needle's wings.
And then I knew, that like the mended net,
I, too, would go by seasons to the sea,
No refuge in my heart for death or fear,
And patch with toil the ravages of grief
Until, from salt and buffeting of tides,
My twine dissolve beneath its weaver's hand.

NANCY CATO

Independence

I will think of the leech-gatherer on the lonely moor.—*Wordsworth.*

How the red road stretched before us, mile on mile
Narrowing into the distance, straight as though ruled

On yellow paper, away to the lilac hills
Low on the horizon. Above them the storm-clouds piled
In a sky blue as though bruised; yet all ahead
Was glowing in an unearthly wash of light—
Dry roly-poly and saltbush lit to beauty,
The sky a menace, but the wide plains bright.

And there in that lonely place an ancient swagman,
Traveller, bagman, sundowner, what you will—
His rolled-up blankets slung aslant his shoulders,
Billy dangling, his back to the line of hills
And the coming storm: as mysterious in that place
(With his hat set straight and his grey beard blowing)
As a small ship glimpsed a moment far from land.
Where did he come from, where could he be going?

I shall never know, for we had to race the rain
That turns the blacksoil plains to a gluey mud
Bogging to the axles. Only a wave of the hand,
But still the imagination glows, the blood
Stirs at the memory of that symbolic stranger
Glimpsed in a moment of vision and swiftly gone:
Man and his independent spirit, alone
On the vast plains, with night and rain coming on.

JAMES McAULEY

Canticle

Stillness and splendour of the night,
When, after slow moonrise,
Swans beat their wings into the height,
Seeking the brilliant eyes
Of water, where the ponds and lakes
Look upward as the landscape wakes.

The loved one, turning to her lover,
Splendid, awake, and still,
Receives as the wild swans go over
The deep pulse of love's will.
She dies in her delight, and then
Renews her tender love again.

Where fragrant irises disclose
A kingdom to the sense,
The ceremony of pleasure goes
With stately precedence;
Like rich brocade it gleams and glooms
Through the heart's dim presence-rooms.

The wagtail in the myrtle-tree
Who cannot sleep for love
Sings all night long insistently
As if his song could prove
What wisdom whispered from the start,
That only love can fill the heart.

He sang under the boughs of youth,
Through twisted shadowed years;
He sings in this clear night of truth,
And now my spirit hears;
And sees, when beating wings have gone,
The lucid outline of the Swan.

Late Winter

The pallid cuckoo
Sent up in frail
Microtones
His tiny scale

On the cold air.
What joy I found
Mounting that tiny
Stair of sound.

At Bungendore

Now the white-buskined lamb
Deserts his ewe and bawls;
The rain spills from the dam;
A far-off bird-cry falls.

So harsh the bough, yet still
The peach-buds burst and shine.
The blossoms have their will;
I would that I had mine:

That earth no more might seem,
When spring shall clot the bough,
Irised by the gleam
Of tears, as it does now.

New Guinea

In memory of Archbishop Alain de Boismenu, M.S.C.

Bird-shaped island, with secretive bird-voices,
Land of apocalypse, where the earth dances,
The mountains speak, the doors of the spirit open,
And men are shaken by obscure trances.

The forest-odours, insects, clouds and fountains
Are like the figures of my inmost dream,
Vibrant with untellable recognition;
A wordless revelation is their theme.

The stranger is engulfed in those high valleys,
Where mists of morning linger like the breath
Of Wisdom moving on our specular darkness:
Regions of prayer, of solitude, and of death!

Life holds its shape in the modes of dance and music,
The hands of craftsmen trace its patternings;
But stains of blood, and evil spirits, lurk
Like cockroaches in the interstices of things.

We in that land begin our rule in courage,
The seal of peace gives warrant to intrusion;
But then our grin of emptiness breaks the skin,
Formless dishonour spreads its proud confusion.

Whence that deep longing for an exorcizer,
For Christ descending as a thaumaturge
Into his saints, as formerly in the desert,
Warring with demons on the outer verge.

Only by this can life become authentic,
Configured henceforth in eternal mode:
Splendour, simplicity, joy—such as were seen
In one who now rests by his mountain road.

Pietà

A year ago you came
Early into the light.
You lived a day and night,
Then died; no one to blame.

Once only, with one hand,
Your mother in farewell
Touched you. I cannot tell,
I cannot understand

137

A thing so dark and deep,
So physical a loss:
One touch, and that was all

She had of you to keep.
Clean wounds, but terrible,
Are those made with the Cross.

HAL PORTER

Lalique

Iris, lilac, lily, milk,
sketched on air and watered silk
the flaxen frozen paddocks lie
beneath the pearl-shell of the sky.

Between the furrows, orchid-white,
shadows green as malachite;
filament river mauve and chill
unspools below a muslin hill.

Scratched-on fences in a net
cobweb-glimmer rainbow-wet;
plumbago mare with frosty mane
winces at the lark-far train.

Chalky shack's still charmed, and yet
chimney smokes a cigarette,
and from the zinc-white roof out-stings
a smack of tin, like glassy wings.

One wink more the blond-scape stays
curved in lalique whorl of haze:
iris, jonquil, fragile, spare,
pricked on silk and champagne air.

Sheep

They teeter with an inane care among the skewbald stones,
plead each other's prison names in grey bewildered tones,
and trust their faces—powdered pale and bilious with unease—
against the wires of the fence, like haunted internees:
"Here and here, man, m-a-a-n."

From off the withers of the slopes the traitor clouds have
    fled
guerrilla wind's philippic and the sun's assault of red;
the mincing, gelded, godless tribe bleats anguish in a haze
of sacrificial tulles of dust and rings of feckless days:
"Here and here, man, m-a-a-n."

Disquieted, illusionless, from jibbahs stuck with twigs,
the visors carved with grieving mourn beneath judicial wigs;
upon their brows in horny pride Ionic head-dress coils,
while eyes, opaque with hankering, roll in their timid oils:
"Here and here, man, m-a-a-n."

About them die the sun-scarred miles, the dams of muddy
    milk,
the fences sutured on mirage, the ranges ripped from silk;
before them, from the gravel road, their murderer assesses,
their Judas peers at haughty teeth and parts their clumsy
    dresses:
"Here and here, man, m-a-a-n."

W. S. FAIRBRIDGE

Consecration of the House

House, you are done. . . .
           And now before
The high contracting parties take
Final possession, let us stand
Silent for this occasion at the door,

Who here a lifelong compact make:
That you were not for trading planned,
Since barter wears the object poor,
But are henceforth our living stake
—And hereunto we set our hand.
  Be over us, be strong, be sure.

You may not keep from world alarms,
But from the daily wind and rain
Of guessed, or real, or of imagined wrong
Shadow us between your arms;
Be our sincere affection, and maintain
A corner here for art and song;
Yet no mere image of benumbing calms,
But a bold premiss, where the mind may gain
Purchase for adventurous journeys long.
  Be round us, and protect from harms.

A roof well timbered, hollow walls
Where the damp creep never comes,
Kiln-hardened joists no worm can bore;
Low sills where early daylight falls
Beneath wide eaves against the summer suns;
Huge cupboards, where a child might store
Surfeit of treasures; and no cramping halls,
But spacious and proportioned rooms;
A single, poured foundation, perfect to the core.
  Be our security against all calls.

Six orange-trees, a lemon, and a passion-vine.
All the lush living that endears
A home be yours: some asters for a show,
And roses by the wall to climb,
Hydrangeas fat as cauliflowers.

We who (how arduously!) have watched you grow,
We feel you in the very soil; and time
Shall tie your flesh with ours, your piers
And pipes intestinal, that anchor you below.
　　Be through us, and prevent our fears.

Your windows face the north: the sun
At four o'clock leaps in;
By breakfast-time has swung so high
We lose him; till upon his downward run,
Swollen and yellow as a mandarin,
We catch his amber from the western sky.
Then when the night's dark web is spun,
Let your glass like a stationary comet gleam,
And lantern to our light supply.
　　Be our sure welcome, and a wakeful beam.

Though we designed and built you, we
Will not outlive what we have done.
And if our children here succeed,
Our gain is now, and yours. Let this mortar be
Consecrate to death—a place where one
Gladly might wither to his glowing seed.
We serve you then in all humility
Who serve us, and by our sweat were won
When we had most need.
　　Give us the obligations that make free.

House, you are done. . . . And nevermore
So painted, new, so arrogantly clean;
The tang of lime, the horrid clang
Of footsteps on the naked floor
Will fade to a serene
Patina of sounds and smells that hang

M

Like the reverberations of a shore
Of history: a hive where love has been,
And whence the future sprang.
　　Be powerful above us all. Be sure.

IAN HEALY

Poems from the Coalfields

I. AIR SHAFT

The hearts are pumping—feel!—the air
Flows down from such an open place,
Flows down the bratticed windpipes
To the face.

The air is flowing—sweet, its breath;
But flows it grimly, for the lungs
Are dusted with the particles of death.

2. ADVICE FROM A NIGHTWATCHMAN

This is no place for lovers;
Find a park.
All I'm afraid this offers
Is the dark—
The dark reminder of a hooter's blow,
The dark adventure of a day below,
The dark and silent outline of a wheel
Against the sky, the dark and clammy feel
Of what can happen down there
In the dark
To him who holds your hand; go
Find a park.

ROSEMARY DOBSON

Methuselah

(From "The Devil and the Angel")

The man was called Methuselah I remember,
I kept a memo folded in my garment;
Having a slight forgetfulness to combat
I arm myself against it.
                                        Thus prepared
I journeyed to his dwelling; now through Heaven,
Cleaving the clouds with mission and importance,
And now on foot, joyful by turns or dreaming;
And dreaming thus I chanced upon the Devil.
"Friend," I said (we observe these small refinements),
"Being met upon a singleness of purpose
We might perhaps continue on together."
"Agreed," he said; "but look, the time is early,
The sun not far advanced beyond the valley;
I have two coins upon me and the path here
Is smooth enough—we'll toss a coin together."
I argued back and forth and then remembered
As well to offer, to accept is courteous.
We tossed a round. The Devil won. Far off, Methuselah,
Somewhat surprised, beyond his span of living,
Begat a son called Lamech. We tossed again,
I won. The chance was even. Meanwhile Methuselah
Turned two, three, then four hundred. Many sons
Rejoiced his age. "Time goes," I cried. The Devil
In silence tossed again. Methuselah
Begat near twenty daughters. "Time," I said to the Devil;
"Time, *please*," I said. He pocketed the pennies.

Methuselah turned to greet us from his deathbed.
And round him half a hundred sons and daughters
Mourned and lamented his departing spirit.

The Raising of the Dead

Moved by the miracles of saints—
The child restored, the leper healed—
Through the black plumes of death I watch
The intervening angels step
Down the blue sky, across the field.

To see the young man raised to life,
The soul return to shuttered eyes
They crowd in faded radiance
Where, underneath an orange-tree,
So inexplicably he lies.

They lift the hand left limp by death
And stir the stiffly painted gown,
The wind of life is on their lips,
The holy gold about their heads:
Thus has the painter set them down.

Angels are free to come and go—
My pity for the youth who lies
These seven centuries at least
Returned to Life; who once had caught
A wink, a glimpse, of Paradise.

Detail from an Annunciation by Crivelli

My sisters played beyond the doorway,
My mother bade me hush and go,
I did not think that any saw me
I went so still on tip of toe.

My sisters played beneath the olives,
They called like birds from tree to tree;
I climbed the stairs and through the archway
Looked where no one else could see.

My hair hung straight beneath my cap,
My dress hung down in fold on fold,
And when the painter filled it in
He edged it round with strokes of gold.

My mother thought I played without,
My sisters thought I stayed within,
Only the painter saw me hide—
His brush held upwards to begin.

I saw the Dove, I saw the Lady
Cross her hands upon her breast,
I heard a music, and a shining
Came upon my eyes to rest.

I am twelve, but I was eight then:
No one listens when I tell—
Least of all my little sisters—
What I saw and what befell.

Look upon the painter's picture,
See, he shows you where I hid,
What I saw, and how I listened—
You believe me that I did?

The Birth

A wreath of flowers as cold as snow
Breaks out in bloom upon the night:
That tree is rooted in the dark,
It draws from dew its breath of life,
It feeds on frost, it hangs in air
And like a glittering branch of stars
Receives, gives forth, its breathing light.

Eight times it flowered in the dark,
Eight times my hand reached out to break
That icy wreath to bear away
Its pointed flowers beneath my heart.
Sharp are the pains and long the way
Down, down into the depths of night
Where one goes for another's sake.

Once more it flowers, once more I go
In dream at midnight to that tree,
I stretch my hand and break the branch
And hold it to my human heart.
Now, as the petals of a rose
Those flowers unfold and grow to me—
I speak as of a mystery.

Across the Straits

Down from his post in the tower
Of glass, concrete, and steel
When daylight drained from the city
He sank like a stone in a well.

The maiden cries in the lift-well
All night for a severed head,
But the doors like knives behind him
Closed on the air instead.

And seven head-scarfed furies
Began to polish and swill
The murderous marbled flooring
To try for his undipped heel.

Oh, there is peril in cities—
But he gained the outermost door

And paused like a swimmer ready
To try for a fabled shore.

And he cried as he cried ever nightly
Aloud to the deities,
"Safe-conduct, gods, to my loved one
Over these battering seas."

As a tumult of waves the traffic
Roared against concrete and steel,
And he cleft through the shoals of impeding
Crowds, and dived under the swell.

She has hung her lit lamp in the window,
She presses her face to the pane,
In a wild commotion of longing
She waits for his coming again.

Oh, there is peril in cities—
He shall not escape as he please,
And Hero shall watch for Leander
In vain on those dark, bitter seas.

GWEN HARWOOD

Panther and Peacock

Professor Eisenbart, with grim distaste,
skirted the laughter of a Sunday crowd
circling an ape's gross mimicry of man.
His mistress watched a peacock. He grimaced,
making rude observations on the proud
creature's true centre of that radiant fan.

Raked by the aureoled bird's nerve-twisting cries
they strolled away, affecting noble ease.

A clot of darkness moved in temperate shade:
a jungle climate, favouring decay,
flared through the keyholes of a panther's eyes
to tarnish the gold gauze of sun, and fade

blue from the brilliant air.
                    "Glutted with leisure
dull-coupled citizens and their buoyant young
gape at your elegant freedom, and my face
closed round the cares of power, see with mean pleasure
age scaling massive temples overhung
with silver mists of hair—that handspan space

corners their destiny: at my word they'll bear
acerebrate hybrid monsters. *Fiat nox!*
Let the dark beast whose cat-light footpads scour
my cortex barren leap from its cage and tear
their feathers out!"
                    His mistress said, "What shocks
await the bourgeois! Now at the twilight hour

the earth blooms velvet-soft, while its immense
authority of volume fails and dies
with the clear colours of substantial day.
Now the sharp iconography of sense
declines to vague abstraction, let your eyes
socket the blaze of Venus, through the play

of leaves in the last branch-caught stir of wings.
Rest here."
                    She cradled his Darwinian head.
Its intricate landscape of fine lines and scars,
ridges and hollows, veins' meanderings,
grew desolate in sleep. Above them spread
a leaf-divided tissue of space and stars.

He dreamed: he walked at sunset through the same
gardens; safe on his tongue the incredible
formula that, spoken, would impel
prodigious ruin. His mistress called his name.
Feathers sprang from the sutures of his skull.
His hands grew rattling quills. As darkness fell

it circumfused worse darkness, in which prowled
familiar nightmare towards him, cowering, gripped
as always fast in horror. A stale breath
of carrion choked him. Fingerless, dewlap-jowled,
bird-beaked, he screamed in silence, and was ripped
awake still rooted in his dream of death.

His mind deep in the vehemence of shade
groped worldwards. Though his body showed no harm,
stone-still, with sorrow frozen on her face
the young girl bent above him. While they made
this strange *pietà*, feathers, glistening warm
with his own heartstain, fell through infinite space.

Prizegiving

Professor Eisenbart, asked to attend
a girls' school speech night as an honoured guest
and give the prizes out, rudely declined;
but from indifference agreed, when pressed
with dry scholastic jokes, to change his mind,
to grace their humble platform, and to lend

distinction (of a kind not specified)
to the occasion. Academic dress
became him, and as he knew. When he appeared
the girls whirred with an insect nervousness,
the Head in humbler black flapped round and steered
her guest, superb in silk and fur, with pride

to the best seat beneath half-hearted blooms
tortured to form the school's elaborate crest.
Eisenbart scowled with violent distaste,
then recomposed his features to their best
advantage: deep in thought, with one hand placed
like Rodin's thinker. So he watched the room's

mosaic of young heads. Blond, black, mouse-brown
they bent for their Headmistress' opening prayer.
But underneath a light (no accident
of seating, he felt sure), with titian hair
one girl sat grinning at him, her hand bent
under her chin in mockery of his own.

Speeches were made and prizes given. He shook
indifferently a host of virgin hands.
"*Music!*" The girl with titian hair stood up,
hitched at a stocking, winked at nearby friends,
and stood before him to receive a cup
of silver chased with curious harps. He took

her hand, and felt its voltage fling his hold
from his calm age and power; suffered her strange
eyes, against reason dark, to take his stare
with her to the piano, there to change
her casual schoolgirl's for a master's air.
He forged his rose-hot dream as Mozart told

the fullness of all passion or despair
summoned by arrogant hands. The music ended,
Eisenbart teased his gown while others clapped,
and peered into a trophy which suspended
his image upside down: a sage fool trapped
by music in a copper net of hair.

GWEN HARWOOD

Last Meeting

Shadows grazing eastwards melt
from their vast sun-driven flocks
into consubstantial dusk.
A snow wind flosses the bleak rocks,

strips from the gums their rags of bark,
and spins the coil of winter tight
round our last meeting as we walk
the littoral zone of day and night,

light's turncoat margin: rocks and trees
dissolve in nightfall-eddying waters;
tumbling whorls of cloud disclose
the cold eyes of the sea-god's daughters.

We tread the wrack of grass that once
a silver-bearded congregation
whispered about our foolish love.
Your voice in calm annunciation

from the dry eminence of thought
rings with astringent melancholy:
"Could hope recall, or wish prolong
the vanished violence of folly?

"Minute by minute summer died;
time's horny skeletons have built
this reef on which our love lies wrecked.
Our hearts drown in their cardinal guilt."

The world, said Ludwig Wittgenstein,
is everything that is the case.
—The warmth of human lips and thighs;
the lifeless cold of outer space;

151

this windy darkness; Scorpio
above, a watercourse of light;
the piercing absence of one face
withdrawn for ever from my sight.

COLIN THIELE

Bert Schultz

Bert Schultz on his West Coast farm
Eases backwards through the doorway of his truck,
And the cabin grows around him, the wheel
Finds comfort in a padded stomach rut.
Bert Schultz in motion is a monstrous forward shoot
Because he crushes the accelerator like a toadstool
Under his six-pound boot.

Bert Schultz on his West Coast farm
Wears braces like railway tracks
That start from button boulders,
Junction in the middle of his back
And climb over the mountains of his shoulders.

Bert Schultz in his West Coast town
Has a fence-post arm to buttress up the bar,
Spins a thimble schooner in the stale-smelling ebb,
Talks about sheep and the way prices are.

The glass hidden in his ham-bone fist,
An hour later he still talks farm,
While the flies tip and veer
In the tangle of the wire sprouting on his arm.

Bert Schultz down a West Coast street
Makes me certain Eyre Peninsula
Has taken to its legs,

And is walking round the place on tree-stump feet;
Makes me feel the steel of yaccas,
And the supple punch of mallee,
And the thirsty tug of eighteen-gallon kegs.

Bert Schultz knows something of tractor oils and sumps,
Sheep dogs and petrol pumps
And an occasional punch to the chin.
But when he laughs like a shaking mountain,
Or gullies his face badly with a grin,
He opens suddenly and lets you in.

Tom Farley

Tom Farley, up to his knees in sheep
By the drafting yard, moves in a red fog
Of summer dust; moves, bent, in a rhythm deep
As the seasons, his hard-soft hands
Holding gentle conversation with his dog.

Tom Farley on his Mid-North run
Has a face as fresh and kindly as his sheep;
Wears an old felt hat with its brim full of sun,
Sees the waves of wool move as soothingly as sleep.

Tom Farley lives a life of moving sheep:
Sheep flowing down the slopes
In broad falls
Or unwinding slowly like slack ropes
From knots at dams;
Cataracts of sheep in flood down ledges
Leaping and bucking in angles and edges,
Tossing up like flotsam the horns of rams;
Sheep held in the hollows and valleys
In friendly lakes rippling gently in the sun
On Farley's run.

And Tom, sometimes caught in the rucking tide
Of backs, feels them break against him,
Carry him forward in their jostle and surge
Till, fingers crooked deep in wool, he wades wide
To the fence and at last stands free
Like a tired surfer plodding from the sea.

But Tom finds himself most deeply once a year
When the sheep-dog trials come to test his dog. . . .

Then, by riddled stump or fallen log
He sucks his pipe and—eyes alight,
Though ringed by the crowsfeet treading round their hol-
    lows—
Sums up the sheep and the brain of the dog that follows;
But when Tom and his noiseless shadow slip
Onto the oval green where the renegade ewes
Fidget and shift, people pity the others' chances
For these two are always surer, a little faster,
Fluid with the knowing talk of nods and glances—
A spiritual union of the dog and master.

Tom Farley and his dog, they say, will wipe
The field—so much at one in paddocks, yards and races
That folk would hardly be surprised
Some day to see them interchange their places,
See the dog stand up to fill his brier pipe,
And old Tom, dropping to the turf behind the flock,
Creep stealthily with feints and cunning graces,
And, nose to the ground, sink his teeth in a lagging hock.

DOROTHY AUCHTERLONIE

Apopemptic Hymn

All was as it was when I went in:
The pictures right-side up, the chairs in place,
The flowers stood stiff upon the mantelpiece,
I knew the voice, I recognized the face.

Outside, the same sky held the same earth fast,
The green leaves shone, dogs barked, the children played;
But suddenly, inside, the air grew cold,
The evening ceased to sing, I was afraid.

The chairs began to dance, the pictures screamed,
The suppurating flowers smelt sickly-sweet,
The white walls clashed together, silence howled,
The floor collapsed in darkness at my feet.

The door slams shut, the wind is in my hair,
The sun has gone, and in its place there stands
The mighty stranger, blotting out the sky;
I turn and feel my way with cold, blind hands.

But where I turn, he stands before me still,
Annihilating time, bestriding space,
Chaos is come, my daughter is unborn,
And blank and featureless my own son's face.

No point of recognition but the grass—
Even the tree betrays me in the end—
Oh blind hands, feel the toughness of the blades
And the cold ground beneath them as your friend.

LEX BANNING

Captain Arthur Phillip and the Birds

Copper-green Phillip
with a beak like a hawk,
perches on his pedestal
and will not talk
to the stuttering starlings
fluttering around
or the crumb-seeking pigeons
patterning the ground;
and though, daylong,
bird calls to bird,
copper-green Phillip
says never a word.

Copper-green Phillip
just stares and stands
with a scroll and a flag
in his strong bronze hands,
and the birds may wonder
what's on the scroll:
is it the *Sirius's*
pilgrims' roll;
or, perhaps, a commission;
or a declaration,
washing his hands
of the subsequent nation;
or, even, an inventory
of flocks and herds?
But Royal Navy captains
never talk to birds.

Copper-green Phillip
just stands and stares
away down the harbour
at the rolling years,

and the birds all gossip
of the nation's vices,
and of some of her virtues,
and of whom she entices
but whether she's Magdalene,
or whether she's Martha,
it's all the same
to Captain Arthur.

MAX HARRIS

The Tantanoola Tiger

There in the bracken was the ominous spoor mark,
Huge, splayed, deadly, and quiet as breath,
And all around lay bloodied and dying,
Staring dumbly into their several eternities,
The rams that Mr Morphett loved as sons.

Not only at Tantanoola, but at Mount Schank
The claw welts patterned the saplings
With mysteries terrible as Egypt's demons,
More evil than the blueness of the Lakes,
And less than a mile from the homestead, too.

Sheep died more rapidly than the years
Which the tiger ruled in tooth and talk,
And it padded from Beachport to the Border,
While blood streamed down the minds of the folk
Of Mount Gambier, Tantanoola, and Casterton.

Oh this tiger was seen all right, grinning,
Yellow and gleaming with satin stripes:
Its body arched and undulated through the tea-tree:
In this land of dead volcanoes it was a flame.
It was a brightness, it was the glory of death:

It was fine, this tiger, a sweet shudder
In the heath and everlastings of the Border,
A roc bird up the ghostly ring-barked gums
Of Mingbool Swamp, a roaring fate
Descending on the mindless backs of grazing things.

Childhoods burned with its burning eyes,
Tantanoola was a magic playground word,
It rushed through young dreams like a river,
And it had lovers in Mr Morphett and Mr Marks
For the ten long hunting unbelieving years.

Troopers and blacks made safari, Africa-fashion;
Pastoral Quixotes swayed on their ambling mounts,
Lost on invisible trails. The red-faced
Young Lindsay Gordons of the Mount
Tormented their heartbeats in the rustling nights

While the tiger grew bigger, and clear as an axe.
"A circus once abandoned a tiger cub"—
This was the creed of the hunters and poets:
"A dingo that's got itself too far south"
The grey old cynics thundered in their beers;

And blows were swapped and friendships broken;
Beauty burst on a loveless and dreary people,
And their monied minds broke into singing
A myth; these soured and tasteless settlers
Were Greeks and Trojans, billabong troubadours,

Plucking their themes at the picnic races
Around the kegs in the flapping canvas booths.
On the waistcoats sharks' teeth swung in time,
And old eyes, sharply seamed and squinting,
Opened mysteriously in misty musical surprise,

Until the day Jack Heffernan made camp
By a mob of sheep on the far slope of Mount Schank,
And woke to find the tiger on its haunches,
Bigger than a mountain, love, or imagination,
Grinning lazily down on a dying ewe;

And he drew a bead and shot it through the head.
Look down, oh mourners of history, poets,
Look down on the black and breeding volcanic soil,
Lean on your fork in this potato country,
Regard the yellowed fangs and quivering claws

Of a mangy and dying Siberian wolf.
It came as a fable or a natural image
To pace the bars of these sunless minds,
A small and unimpressive common wolf
In desperately poor and cold condition.

It howled to the wattle when it swam ashore
From the wreck of the foundered *Helena*,
Smelt death and black snakes and tight lips
On every fence-post and slip-rail.
It was three foot six from head to tail.

Centuries will die like swatted blowflies
Before word of wolf will work a tremor
Of tenderness in the crusty knuckles
Around the glasses in the Tantanoola pub
Where its red bead eyes now stare towards the sun.

Martin Buber in the Pub

My friends are borne to one another
By their lack of something to say;
The weight of inward thought is lifted
And they float to each other

Like paper darts: they offer the salt of themselves
Arab-like in hotels,
Humbler than they would have you believe.
Humanity is the smallest coin for tipping.
Alan relates a host of grandiose lies. . . .
These are the wafers of our religion.
Barnes is the butt of malice,
An unmysterious drinking of the blood. . . .

And the seas may boil outside. No doubt they do.
But we are in a silence of some sort,
Exchanging shells, which placed against the ear,
Occasionally echo the throbbing of a heart.

NAN McDONALD

The White Eagle

Evening falls soon in the hills across the river,
Moving dark where the tree-tops gleamed a moment before,
Chilling to steel the lazy sweep of the reaches,
And at last, salt-cold, comes rippling in to our shore,

Where the gulls long since wheeled up and went flashing
    seaward,
With the tide's first ebb deserting the threatened land;
And the shag no longer sits where the bleaching driftwood
Thrusts from the slate-blue mud and damp white sand.

And the shadow climbs, and the clamorous gold-green
    thickets
Grow shrill with a brief unease that falls dulled to rest;
The thrush drops his gentle head, as in secret listening
To the freshets of silver locked in his soft grey breast.

And the lyre-bird too, that gay and skilful fellow,
Who set the dawn-fogged dew of the bush alight
With the opal glow of his soul and his art's rich cunning,
Can find no song for this other grey of night.

Now far and steeply above us the dusk has swallowed
The glint of the wiry grass that the boulders strew,
Echoing no more to the thronged black currawongs' calling
Where the rose-limbed trees twist out to pattern the blue.

But the light turns blazing at bay in its last high fortress
And the walls of yellow sandstone with glory run,
A crown for the night-gulfed slopes, and a golden footstool
For the lord of the rocks and the champion of the sun.

Stainless he rides on the swimming air, and below him
Roll the vast dim sea and the splendour of the world;
And the strength of his wing will be gilded, his breast still
    blinding
When the citadel falls with its blackened banners furled.

Tomorrow I too must be dropping down the river
With the screams of the flickering gulls for my parting
    words,
And in the thick town I shall be often thinking
Of the great hill darkening here, and my quiet birds.

I shall wish them all a still dusk and safe dreaming,
But the lift of my heart will follow my shining one
Where the high bright cliffs rise burning, and he beyond
    them,
All his white beauty warm in the eye of the sun.

The Hatters

The hut in the bush of bark or rusty tin,
The feel of eyes watching, willing you to be gone;
Here lives a hatter. He has done with the world.
Whatever it was in the end he could not bear—
To look in the face of lecher and fool and see
Himself; the rub of the mask on bleeding skin;
The heavy yoke of God, daily put on,
To endure all things and give back love again—
He has chosen the bush, its simpler cruelty,
Its certain peace. I, too, could break the snare,
Take the hatter's path, say no to God and men. . . .
Yet from such an end, good Lord, deliver me.

My grandfather, riding down Araluen way,
A young man then—it is eighty years and more
Since the rocks of those wild hillsides shone for him
In the yellow sun, and the singing river ran
Clear over nuggets of gold—passed carelessly
The humpy hidden in vines from the bright day
And a hatter fired at him from the dark of the door.
Solemn thought—at least, to me, you may laugh if you will—
That if his aim had been better I should not be.
More solemn, that in the end, between man and man,
There is no choice but this: to love or kill.
From the blood of my brother, Lord, deliver me.

Another lived in the sandhills, a sea-lulled hollow,
And raised a sign to ward off peering eyes:
"Beware of the lion." Any trick was fair against them
But I think he believed it, had seen at morning there
On the rippled beach, through the fine-pricked tracery
Of crab and bird, strange tracks he dared not follow:
Or at twilight, when the silver dune-grass sighs,

162

Had seen the tawny sand, that slept all day
Warm and quiet, rise up now, move stealthily
About his hut. Still he cries to me, "Beware!
Beware the beast that lurks along this way!"
From the claws of madness, Lord, deliver me.

And in the mountains behind Jamberoo,
The bush dead still at noon, clouds hanging low,
I came on a hut, close barred, the windows darkened,
On its door one word: "Silence!" And all around
A hush so deep no sound, it seemed, could be
Unwelcome—the shriek of a black cockatoo
Though it boded storm, the hungry cry of a crow,
Even human speech, so rare in that lost place.
I did not knock; I had no wish to see
One who desired a silence more profound.
What hand would have opened to me there? What face?
From the love of death, dear Lord, deliver me.

PETER BLADEN

Coronation Day at Melrose

It was quite a day at Melrose. All the folks had come to town
  there
And they gathered at the schoolhouse, but the teacher didn't
  frown there;
And they squeezed into the kiddies' seats, but not for sums
  or spelling.
There were prayers devoutly offered, there were fervent
  anthems welling.
Yes—"The King of love my shepherd is" . . . the words in
  beauty sounding,
While the people bowed in homage, and in joyfulness
  abounding.

In the sunshine then they gathered, and the echoes of a bell
rose
Where the people lifted up their hearts and pledged them-
selves at Melrose.

Next they held a gay procession; there were streamers, flags
and bunting,
And the larger girls wore costumes made with little room
for grunting;
While the smaller fry were cowboys, or they sported whop-
ping noses,
And their little sisters dressed like ladies—frills and lace and
roses.
With a drum and rusty bugles came the band. Another star
thing
Was the chap who rode a home-made gadget called a "penny-
farthing"!
There were soldiers at attention, and at last a happy yell rose
When the crowd beheld the glitter of the smiling Queen of
Melrose.

The procession broke in half because a truck had lost its
driver,
But they laughed, while they were waiting, at the draught-
horse and Godiva;
There were floats with baby napkins, minstrels, little maids-
in-waiting,
And a barrow-load of clowns and pretty prams, perambu-
lating.
Through the gateway to the oval, with a picnic feast to mop
off—
And a truck was stuck beneath the gate until they took its
top off.

It was lunchtime, and quite pleasing when a most delicious
    smell rose:
There were Coronation patties at the old hotel at Melrose.

In the afternoon the football . . . they decided to burlesque it,
Men in girls' kit, girls in men's kit, mostly all in one-big-
    mess kit!
There were whistles, shouts and shoving, and it left them
    whole, but holey,
And by accident a ball or two would trespass past the goalie.
Oh, they played and laughed and sported, and their spirits
    mounted higher,
Till they almost reached the summit of the near-by Mount
    Maria.
And though others climbed up Everest, or marched in gay
    and swell rows,
Yet their hearts were just as fervent in the little town of
    Melrose.

It was Coronation Day. Oh yes—the day was surely gala,
In the streets and in the playgrounds, in the kitchen, and
    the parlour;
There was little time for anything excepting the rejoicing,
And the things they said at Melrose were the words the
    world was voicing.
So they toasted her, the Princess, who was born to be their
    ruler;
(And a few went toasting near enough to land them in the
    cooler!)
Then the sunset came in beauty, like a flush of softest shell-
    rose;
Coronation Day was over in the little town of Melrose.

Variations on a Medieval Theme

Strong, but with gentleness,
Young, but womanly,
She weights with wantonness
Her guarded beauty.

Her eyes are all earth's colours
Flickering in her face,
Whose flesh with bone concurs
In one perfect embrace.

No other colours she uses,
Her lips are their own red,
She is kind, refuses
Me nothing, not even her bed.

But distance now defeats
The image that I see.
Sweetest under all sheets
She lies where I cannot be.

January

In summer when the hills are blond
O dark-haired girl with wave-wet ankles
Bare your skin to the sun and to me.
All summer go brown, go salt by the sea.

O dark-haired girl stay close to me
As grass that shivers on the hill's hot flank
Or your spine that trembles under my hand;
The pale grass is dead, but not so the sea.

Across the paddocks stooks and bales
In separate civilizations stand
Like tribesmen's tents and townsmen's cities,
While a dark girl swims in distant seas.

The sun's blond fire turns red and black,
A horrible army runs through hay
By flank of hill through hair of tree
And the ashes fall upon the sea.

Stook-tents, bale-cities all fall down
And fences keep the dead stock back.
O dark-haired girl, stay close to me,
All summer go brown, go salt by the sea.

ALEXANDER CRAIG

Hillside

1

A shed in blue-grey weatherboard with a high
Red roof, between the low pale apple-trees,
And a cluster of dark pines brushing the sky

Show half-way up the hill and seem to seize
Me as a painting might. The orchard-squares
Patterning their slope set even my mind at ease.

Faint rain-mist softens detail now. Well, there's
The scene and its slight movement. . . Night and rain
Will end it, busy with their own affairs.

2

Memento mori: evening brings again
With its subtle sullen undertone a grey
Sky-shroud that wraps my world, brings the inane

167

Sameness of each coming night, each day
Dying in darkness, till at last we are
Caught in a darkness from which no man may

Conjure or kindle even a single star
To peep through a window of his last long home.
I stare out through my windowpane, and far

Across the hidden hillside now there come
Cat's-eyes from crouching houses, winking light
Mocking the planets circling the sky's dome

Seen in their stately march on a calm night.
The great blade of the wind will scythe for miles
The tall rain growing downward from its height.

3

And now the icecream clouds the morning piles
On the wide plate of the horizon please the child
In me a moment: the metaphor beguiles

The grown man less because I know their mild
And foaming mass holds rain as sharp as nails,
And wounded birds will scud across the wild

Inverted sea with ineffectual sails,
Storm-driven, harried, sinking from the sky.
But I am wrong: sun shines; the sky unveils

The blue-grey wooden shed again—its high
Red roof of tin—the pale-green apple-trees,
The dark sky-brushing pine-trees too, that I

Saw yesterday. Cars move in twos and threes
Along the horizon, past the castellated
Brick grocer's on White's Corner, over these.

4

This air, this vessel of light, is self-created,
Suffusing all the midday in its glow
And pouring on the midnight still its fated

And tragic sense of longing. It is as though
Our images, returning to their source,
Took on their own life: objects that I know

Shine with a strange clearness and new force
In that familiar element. Shed and tree,
Caught in that tide of time, arrest its course

Whose good and evil no man can foresee.

NANCY KEESING

Revelation

Observe this man, he is an engineer;
Notice his useful hands; his eyes are keen.
He has spent his life in the designing
And service—and faithful love—of the machine.

All joy for him existed in smooth surface,
Music was in the purr of a good flywheel,
A satisfactory evening's conversation
Concerned the nice efficiency of steel.

We can assume that it was business that forced him
To drive down the Windsor road at the end of the day
When, for an hour, the landscape is sharply focussed
Before night smooths each long contour away.

With every mile the mountains close on the traveller
Who, with a sudden, a wholly astonishing vision
Finds they are part of a plan, an entire conception
Terrifying in its harmony and precision.

His sight, being trained only to see essentials,
Can strip the trees from the hills and the moss from the
    boulders
Revealing the ultimate anatomy,
Spreading away from the plateau's stony shoulders.

A mind that had thought too long in terms of blueprint
Discovered affinity with the slopes and the plain,
Losing itself in technical admiration
Of this enormous provision for stress and strain. . . .

Perhaps he came again, I cannot tell you;
But this I know, his eyes proclaim a change.
He can touch his machines, but has no comfort from them,
The oily wheels are meaningless and strange.

Not that he views the world as a machine;
Nevertheless, he is an engineer
And, having known perfection for an hour,
Lives all his hours in beauty—and in fear.

One could expect that. Hoping to find solutions
In man's small science and his vast defeat,
While the strength thus sought, and tested by the ages,
Rests in the earth, absolute and complete.

Bread

I make man's ancient food
That at blood's temperature
Gathered its own life,
Began to seethe and stir.

I plunge my fists within
Resilient dough for bread,
The living, leavened stuff
Fragrant and moist to knead

Takes shape now from my hand,
Its warmth of growing yeast
Springs from the palm pressed in
And curls back to resist.

My atavistic hands
Find an old skill to throw
And press and curve and turn
And shape the living dough.

I set the bread to rise
And hear the smallest sound
Beneath the muslin cloth
That covers it around.

It is the sound of life
From dough that warmed the hand
And took blood's heat to grow.
I shape the loaves, they stand

Again to rise before
Their baking into food—
Bread that is symbol of
Plain goodness, life and God.

All generations of women
Who ground the flour for bread,
And set it by their ovens
And curved strong hands to knead,

How intimately they knew
Whence man's true symbols come:
The seed, the yeast, the bread,
The child swelling the womb.

ERIC ROLLS

Sheaf-tosser

The lone crow caws from the tall dead gum:
Caw. Caw. Caw-diddle-daw.
And judges the stack with one watery eye,
Then turns the other to fix its lie.
Caw. Caw. Caw-diddle-daw.
There are four tiers of sheaves on the wagon yet
And one more loaded is standing by;
My arms are aching and I'm dripping sweat
But the sun is three axe-handles in the sky
And I must toss sheaves till dark.

It is fourteen feet from the ground to the eaves:
Caw. Caw. Caw-diddle-daw.
And two feet six to the third roof row,
Six feet high stands the load below:
Caw. Caw. Caw-diddle-daw.
Ten feet six now must I pitch,
Into the centre of the stack I throw
To the turner and the short-handled fork with which
He thrusts sheaves to the builder in monotonous flow,
Butts out and long-side down.

There are twenty-five crows on the old dry gum:
Caw. Caw. Caw-diddle-daw.
Thirteen on one branch and twelve on the other
And each one calls as loud as his brother,

Caw. Caw. Caw-diddle-daw.
My hands are blistered, my sore lips crack
And I wonder whether the turner would smother
If a hard throw knocked him off the stack
And a few sheaves slipped on top? But there'd come another
And I'd still toss sheaves.

There are thousands of crows on the gaunt white gum:
Caw. Caw. Caw-diddle-daw.
The reds are pale in the western sky
And the stack is more than sixty feet high:
Caw. Caw. Caw-diddle-daw.
My fork grows heavy as the light grows dim.
There are five sheaves left but I've fear of a whim
That one of the crows has an evil eye
And the five sheaves left will be there when I die,
For each bird's forgotten how to fly
Till he drives out my soul with the force of his cry:
Caw. Caw. Caw. Caw.
Caw. Caw. Caw. Caw.

Little Sticks

I made my fire of little sticks
And thought to sit beside it.
It burned so hot it melted bricks
And all the chimney ran away
In a twisting line of molten clay
And warmth rode out astride it.

There is awful power in little things.
Last week I filled my billy
Where the water outward springs
Down the mountain making creeks.
I made a fire of little sticks.
The water boiled up silly.

O

I threw the tea on a bursting bubble;
Tapped the leaves well down.
No tea I had for all my trouble;
It burned too hot and wouldn't cool
So I hooked it over the spring-filled pool
On a wattle-branch drooped down.

Today, as I was riding there,
Thought of the well-brewed billy.
It dangled empty in the air
With the bottom melted cleanly out
And all around the steam did spout.
The pool was bubbling silly.

I'll build my book as the fire was made
And, if I make it right,
With word and thought as carefully laid
And a sometimes happy kick apart,
Then may it leap and catch a heart
And set it burning bright.

DAVID ROWBOTHAM

Mullabinda

A fig-tree, a falling woolshed, a filled-in well:
The acute corners of one man's figure of hell. . . .
When the tree was young and the well deep and the shed
Mullabinda, these three and Campbell's sheep
Were Campbell's pride—before this northern sweep
Of channelling shallows marked the Queensland-side;
Before death speared and drained the day to dark,
And Campbell, riding home, heard no dog bark.

His broad and glaring mare snorted at the ford
And splashed cold fear into his eyes and beard
With hooves restlessly obedient and ominous.
Upstream, on the highest bank, through the blowing rows
Of wind-break coolabahs, the cypress pine
Of Mullabinda, slabbed between the shine
And pillared strength of bloodwood, rose a violence,
A smokeless shock of fortress stormed by silence.

He heeled the mare to the gallop in his heart.
"Keep clear of the trees, close to the house. At night
Bar the door and open to no stranger,"
He had said, then kissed away the rape of danger
In her eyes, and (gently), "Take the gun to the well
And when you water the fig." A voice replied, "I will. . . ."
Inside the coolabahs the broad mare shied,
And a wind struck through and broke down Campbell's
     pride.

"I found my wife murdered at the well,
The boy with a bucket in his hand and a spear
In his back beside the fig, the girl on a chair
In the house, clubbed like a little animal.
I beg Your Excellency's kind permission to kill.
I remain Your Excellency's humble servant—Campbell."
The graves were heaped, and the special licence came,
And Mullabinda Campbell rode after game.

The target-circles of black breasts, glistening, hung
Thick-nipple-centred over the billabong,
And paddling and playing in pools of water and sun,
The piccaninnies turned plump bellies to the gun,
Teasing the tiny apex of the steely sight. . . .
The legends ricochetted with each report;
Till stone thoughts filled the well of his heart, and age
Made a crumbling woolshed of his slab-hard rage.

Time grooved him like the bloodwood; but deep in the dried
And channelled country of his being where pride
Once flooded to the full, whispered and grew the fig-tree,
Fruitless, but a wild, green and rooted memory,
Growing on, long after the vengeful spear,
Thumping his shoulders out of the quiet air,
Acquitted him of hate, and of tree, shed, well—
Mullabinda Campbell's estimate of hell.

The Town

Like any grey old-timer droving dreams
Across the inland of the past he tramped in,
Now his looking-back desire, this town,
I think, pines for the bark huts that it camped in;

For its billy-tea and damper days, the sound
Of bullock-wagons rumbling through its mornings,
And squatters riding by and station-hands
Playing cards beneath its shanty awnings.

I half expect it shall some day arise,
Puff one last cloud of smoke in its decision
And walk away among the hills and find
Another camp-fire closer to its vision.

THEA ASTLEY

Droving Man

She might have chosen cities, but the man
Compelled to see the pastures of his soul
Stocked with dream cattle,
Moved north and west and sunwards to his goal
Under the freckled lightning of the wattle.

Over the years the piccaninny thoughts
And timid lubra words became so shy
Of their own thunder,
They never spoke together but his eye
Would find in hers a startled twin of wonder.

VINCENT BUCKLEY

Late Tutorial

The afternoon dark increases with the clock
And shadows greening on the cabinet.
Teacher of youth, and more than half a fool,
How should you catch those shadows in your net?

Outside, the world's late colour calls us home:
Not to the refuge of familiar art
Nor house of settling wood, but to the first
Home, to the savage entry of the heart.

There, where the dry lips are cooled with words
And every hand worships the love it serves,
Perhaps we'll find some comfort: the deep spring
Rising, and soft renewal of the nerves

In poetry with its constant singing mouth.
Open the door, then; numbed with winter air,
They smile, and move inside; the colours fade
Ringing my head; they seat themselves, and stare.

So I must learn that these, the learners, come
To teach me something of my destiny;
That love's not pity, words are not mine alone,
And all are twined on the great central tree.

How shall I answer them, give ultimate name
To the nerves at war, the mind in dishabille?
Better to pace with the slow clock, and teach them
Quibbles with which to meet adversity.

Their thoughts come, slow, from a cold bed. Their needs
Are close to me as the smell of my own flesh.
Their timid guesses grow, soft-fallen seeds,
To grace my mind with pain. And should I say

    "O man is sick, and suffering from the world,
    And I must go to him, my poetry
    Lighting his image as a ring of fire,
    The terrible and only means I have;

    "And, yet, I give too much in rhetoric
    What should be moulded with a lifetime's care,
    What peace alone should strike, and hear vibrate
    To the secret slow contraction of the air,"

The talk would die in loud embarrassment,
The books be rustled, and the noses blown
In frenzy of amazement at this short
Still youthful puppet in academic gown.

I cannot, but speak measured foolish words:
Shelley was fitful, Keats a dozing fire.
Pass with the light, poor comrades. You and I
Follow but feebly where our words aspire.

Various Wakings

    Light wake early in this house;
    Blackened pot, and roof, and chain,
    Walls and light-encroaching mouse,

All be trampled by that grace;
Tortured woman, tortured man,
Turn within your spirit's space,
Waking into daily pain.

The pine-trees cast their opening shade
And birds walk in the summer grass;
Curtains are drawn, the breakfast laid.
Outside again, the pain will call
Her body to its desperate pass,
And he with strangling hands will curse
The flight of bees from wall to wall.

Bone of my bone, whose kinship is
The shield of anguish on my breast,
Metal or stone engaging this
Beginning of our light, O seek
In their grave meeting common rest;
And do not fear the common task
That burns the tortured and the meek.

O light be powerful in this house;
Surely the night of common things
Is not so stern that it will rouse
Their creaking bones into a world
That's drained of all imaginings:
Man's image of himself is called
Back from his dream, when morning sings.

And, Wind of my adoring, come
Under the vine-leaves to their heart.
Some serve by exultation, some
Burn in a galaxy of fears.
Teach me one cry, or word, or art
That under the enfeebled stars
They may feel happy and at home.

LAURENCE COLLINSON

The Sea and the Tiger

The sea sucks in the traveller,
indifferent to his frantic thought;
no more vindictive than a stone
it yet destroys the mite it caught.

The craving tiger seeks no man
where animal will do instead;
it cares not what the flesh be from,
nor whether living, whether dead.

And friends, who plan no cruelty,
without deliberation rise
and drown me with their deeds, and with
their honest mouths eat out my eyes.

J. R. ROWLAND

Canberra in April

Vast mild melancholy splendid
Day succeeds day, in august chairmanship
Presiding over autumn. Poplars in valleys
Unwavering candleflames, balance over candid
Rough-linen fields, against a screen of hills

Sending invisible smokes from far below
To those majestic nostrils. A Tuscan landscape
On a larger scale; for olives eucalypts
In drifts and dots on hillheads, magpie and crow
For fieldbirds, light less intimate, long slopes stripped

Bare of vine or village, the human imprint
Scarcely apparent; distances immense
And glowing at the rim, as if the land
Were floating, like the round leaf of a water-plant
In a bright meniscus. Opposite, near at hand,

Outcrops of redbrick houses, northern trees
In costume, office-buildings
Like quartz-blocks flashing many-crystalled windows
Across the air. Oblivious, on their knees,
Of time and setting, admirals pick tomatoes

In their back gardens, hearty
Bankers exchange golf-scores, civil servants
Their after-office beers; the colony
Of diplomats prepares its cocktail parties
And politicians their escape to Melbourne.

This clean suburbia, house-proud but servantless
Is host to a multitude of children
Nightly conceived, born daily, riding bikes,
Requiring play-centres, schools and Progress
Associations: in cardigans and slacks

Their mothers polish kitchens, or in silk
White gloves and tight hats pour each other tea
In their best china, canvassing the merits
Of rival plumbers, grocers, Bega milk
And the cost of oil-fired heating or briquettes.

To every man his car; his wife's on Thursday
Plus one half-day she drops him at the office
(Air murmurous with typewriters) at eight-forty
To pick him up for lunch at home; one-thirty
Sees the streets gorged with his return to duty

And so the year revolves; files swell, are closed
And stored in basements, Parliaments adjourn
And reassemble, speeches are made and hooted.
Within the circle of the enfranchised
These invite those and are themselves invited,

At formal dinners, misprints of the *Times*
Compete with memories of Rome or Paris
For, after all, the capital is here.
The general populace sprays its roses, limes
Its vegetable patch and drinks its beer:

Golf at the week-end, gardening after five
Pictures on Saturday, radio day and night
T.V. to come, and shopping late on Friday—
As under glass the pattern of the hive
Swarms in its channels, purposeful and tidy

Tempting romantics to dismay and spite
Planners to satisfaction, both to heresy:
For everywhere, beyond the decent lawn
A visionary landscape wings the sight
And every child is rebel and unknown.

So long as daylight moon, night laced with stars
And luminous distance feed imagination
There's hope of strangeness to transcend, redeem
Purblind provincial comfort: summer fires
Under prodigious smokes, imperious storms,

A sense of the pale curving continent
That, though a cliché, may still work unseen
And, with its script of white-limbed trees, impart
A cure for habit, some beneficent
Simplicity or steadiness of heart.

Idyll

At noon the sun puffed up, outsize.
We saw a township on the rise;
Jack croaked, "A pub", then filed his throat,
Spat out an encroaching horde of flies.

One-headed Cerberus near the door
Bit off the fag-end of a snore,
Allowed us a red eye's filmy grace
And veiled the awful sight once more.

Sad barman showed a yellow fang;
Sweat was dirt-cheap, the whole place rang
As six-foot told a ten-foot yarn;
One chap was under, and one sang.

I'd bottle up that song without
A license, just to serve it out,
A ballad, long and cool for days
Of epics, dry canteens and drought.

We shouldered through the cork-tipped fog,
Paid several zacks and downed the grog;
Then like the brown fox of copperplate
Made exit over the lazy dog.

A Papuan Shepherd

(From *A Drum for Ben Boyd*)

Through the thick morning steam they took shape,
With fierce white symbols shaking above them in air:
Sea-monsters from icy regions bringing cold tides with them.
Some of us trembled and clapped hands slowly in fear,

While others fingered their spears and stones in doubt;
But when flame sprang, and spirits squeaked overhead
And an incredible thunder troubled the trees,
We crouched in terror lest our sky drip blood.

And then the men with bloodless brittle faces,
With ferocious prayers, solemn and rhythmical,
Seized many of us, the young and the virile,
Dragging us through the surf to impure burial

In the bellies of their tamed monsters.
                                        So we saw
Our gods fall back defeated to the green lands
Fading into mist, leaving us to struggle
With rages and subtleties that no one understands.

Out in these bare places a poison wrings
Power from my arms; each new night spits ice,
And I am forgetting the songs and the careless fishing,
The old fighting and the old peace.

The Room

(From *Leichhardt in Theatre*)

There may be agony in furnished rooms:
Rather, they are its perfect setting. Walls
Clamp down on motive, and the flesh of motive
Puffs up whiter in prominence. The rage
Contracted in the mirror, the sea passion
Trembling in the painted shell, the dust
Beating under the suction of loose curtains:
These the reflection, struggle, witless pacing
Of the man in the furnished room. The neat montage
Of flawless lamplight gathers in his movements;

Exact, predictable as waves, his thoughts
Shatter themselves between the bedstead's knuckles.
Therefore we bring the Doctor to this room.

Peers long into the glass and sees himself
As for the first time, stained and vulnerable,
Branded with whispers. Steeply he rebels,
Curses Mann, Perry, and the merciless rain:
Till something laughs behind him, and he breaks.

Fingers the painted shell. Its surface smooth
Though marred by countless pores; below the light
A shadow slides from the lip, draws in a little.
Always withdrawn, the enigmatic thing
That mocks him: once with lineaments of water,
Again, a girl's face, or a monument,
But now no semblance, ache without the symbol
—Or a gaunt symbol, to be shuddered from.

Moves to the window, stares at eddying dust,
And thinks of dust. Of Gilbert. The pale face
Stamped by the marvellous speed, and covered quickly
Because the eyes were open, shows itself.
Has Gilbert found the source? or do his bones,
Forever at war with death,
Trudge nightly towards Port Essington, till dawn
Chains them again to stone?
                                        A question stares
Relentless from the dust, the answer traces
Legends of fright upon his brain, he turns
Swiftly back to the mirror and, as one
Aloof, for a moment watches fear at work.

But now they close round him in the room:
The question eats its way until the heart

Crumbles beneath its golden arrogance
And he must answer.
                              Savage and at bay!
Fronting the mirror and the tamed grey hound
Whimpering in the glass: "No back is broken
Under a rod of lies." The painted shell:
"Deception is all distance to the sea."
Still, still, the dust. "Shall a man go crazy for the kiss
Of thirst upon his throat? Shall he explore
Time after time this death's-head continent,
Probe the eye-sockets, skinless cavities,
Till the brain sweats from his skull, his hands contract,
And bone probes bone at length; bone lifted to cheek
Knows the flesh dwindling, blasted by such a love?"

Falls silent and betrayed. The walls slope out,
Space bunts at the doorway. Wash of darkness
Save for three shining things. The Furies circle:
Desert with bleached eyes, mountain with the hawk's mouth,
Sea with her witching falseness; cordon him.
He is taken, stripped, and bound.

The Sea

Mile and mile and mile; but no one would gather
That we are running from something; peremptory hours
Examine, order, condemn; all the stars patter together,
A heathen tongue, while our homesick storytelling fires
Are Hellas mouthing, burning;
Little dangerous men attack without warning;
We loot and kill, singing hopelessly in the foreign morning.

And the guide from Gymnias—none of us trusts him, but
    here
We kick anthills, villages tickling his queasy city;
At fear's uplifted finger, fear ravages fear.

186

Ghosts of an army, of a people, how might we have pity
Pity is none of our pain
As, dutifully, dully, we prod blaze for bone.
Talents wink witlessly as we shamble on.

And counterfeit silver on the dry salt leaves of his promise;
Still, in profile, he is our medal of the kill.
See, the sun's withers, letting blood, inform us
Of frightened villages past this giant hill.
—But new rioting overhead:
The little dangerous men? Let us double up to our dead
As the tail of the serpent lashes back to his battered head.

Chorus, tempest, O canting heavy cruse of oil . . .
The sea! And this bay, a carved golden gymnasium
With alarums of the coastal birds that dip and wheel:
Famous, jockeying, muscular, the waves come
Putting their silver weights
Of spray so vehemently. Genesis of lights!
Odysseus begs and prays his passage through the gates.

We call, we fall on our knees, and we embrace.
But Zeus, but Zeus, it is lungs, a living tongue:
These years are resolved in the shapely lips of peace.
Dead men of Melos enter, carefree and young,
To wash all blood from our hands.
We raise an altar of stones; the chanting winds
Fret godly cliff-face for yellow coin of sands.

And our guide? stockstill, the half-smile, the dumb anger.
Something is lost to him, finding itself at the breast.
But something makes obeisance with rings for that thin
    finger,
A horse, a goblet, money. Something may not rest:
Tatterdemalion—see—
Ten thousand ghosts flutter after him. And we
Turn again to our mother, our revels. The sea, the sea!

FRANCIS WEBB

Five Days Old

(For Christopher John)

Christmas is in the air.
You are given into my hands
Out of quietest, loneliest lands.
My trembling is all my prayer.
To blown straw was given
All the fullness of Heaven.

The tiny, not the immense,
Will teach our groping eyes.
So the absorbed skies
Bleed stars of innocence.
So cloud-voice in war and trouble
Is at last Christ in the stable.

Now wonderingly engrossed
In your fearless delicacies,
I am launched upon sacred seas,
Humbly and utterly lost
In the mystery of creation,
Bells, bells of ocean.

Too pure for my tongue to praise,
That sober, exquisite yawn
Or the gradual, generous dawn
At an eyelid, maker of days:
To shrive my thought for perfection
I must breathe old tempests of action.

For the snowflake and face of love,
Windfall and word of truth,
Honour close to death.
O eternal truthfulness, Dove,

Tell me what I hold—
Myrrh? Frankincense? Gold?

If this is man, then the danger
And fear are as lights of the inn,
Faint and remote as sin
Out here by the manger.
In the sleeping, weeping weather
We shall all kneel down together.

NOEL MACAINSH

Kangaroo by Nightfall

The kangaroo by the roadside,
Standing like a milestone
In a place of national pride,
Is changing into shadows,
In fact, it's almost overgrown.

Soon, we'll be able to say—
I think it's still there,
Or perhaps nearer your way—
I think so, but it might have moved;
I can't be sure, it must be somewhere.

And then, of course, everywhere
Will have something of kangaroo—
Shrubs will have ears, a mild stare
Be felt from an empty bush,
And last, wary of what you do,
Of dim trees that could be a hide,
Your heart will thump away from you.

P

Cow Dance

I came across her browsing on a slope
Thatched with dry brown fern scythed in a day
Between milkings, the stones hid in each clump
Blunting the brush-hooks' blades, clanging back
Unhuman oaths over the hill's shoulder
In a noon crackling with summer's fierce wit.
There, mooning and nosing about the grass-tops
Chaffed with holocausts of laughing flame
Or full of chuckling juice mellow as mead,
With an inward jolt at sudden confrontation
She looked up fixedly with liquid eyes
Wide as the stretch of innocence that holds
Pellets of gamin treachery, eyes full of
Remorseless motherhood and blind foraging,
With her two stomachs quite outwitting love,
Lust even, in the common faith
Of bull and cowdom: tyranny of gut.
Being on the loose for laughs, I ran at her
And watched her bolt, all belly and backside
With teats like bagpipes slung beneath a bronco,
For she exploded then, a milk-filled grenade
Gone careering down the slope to the others
Watching her progress with the same wet eyes
Till off they all went, down the hill together,
Horns down, hoofs up, harridans gone dancing
Hell for leather; and, as much a part of the dance,
Centaur-wise I followed in the wake
Of the heifers, leaping down those summer slopes,
Laughing, shouting, mad with the fun of it all.

'Morning, Morning

Soft crying of the dawn while cockatoos
Kark their delight with beating wings, white
And threshing in the kurrajong. In the blue,
The changing glass, a hawk delights
The hanging sun, with soaring dances;
And the brown horse treads the morning dew,
Shakes his red mane, and in the shaking prances.

I don't often see you morning:
No use a lie-abed fellow pretending:
I hold warm the bed. No light comes crawling
Through the dark curtains, no early ending
To my long night. I don't hear the calling
And dancing of cockatoo-crested morning.

At a Time

At a time when love and love
was more than I could bear to give
she cried out, "Then I'm alone,
lonely in the world, alone."

As I stood beside the bay
that the sun set burning bright
she cried tears into my hand,
all I offered was my hand.

I explained the fact of love,
the minute thing that humans have,
but I stumbled on her name;
confused her own, her own pet-name.

Suddenly, a midnight swan
treading white the water sun

rose up and made his own the air,
truly took the trembling air.

Suddenly, most moved by love
I raised her face to see it move,
and we kissed as lovers kiss.
Why remember more than that?

Love and Marriage

Desire that all men have is all my love.
But the girl reads magazines with glossy covers,
Denies the self-in-time that she might have,
Declares that she needs love and never lovers.

Habitual's the thing I most despise.
But the girl talks home and marriage, licensed lovers,
Denies the act, the play, the hope of prize,
Declares she needs what never love discovers.

I should have known, those loving-days ago,
The girl in her hid woman and not lover
For when we fell upon the floor to crow
She saw the carpet needed sweeping over

Though she said nothing then; I had my way.
But she it is who names the wedding-day.

PETER PORTER

Phar Lap in the Melbourne Museum

A masterpiece of the taxidermist's art,
Australia's top patrician stares
Gravely ahead at crowded emptiness.
As if alive, the lustre of dead hairs,

Lozenged liquid eyes, black nostrils
Gently flared, otter-satin coat declares
That death cannot visit in this thin perfection.

The democratic hero full of guile,
Noble, handsome, gentle Houyhnhnm
(In both Paddock and St Leger difference is
Lost in the welter of money)—to see him win
Men sold farms, rode miles in floods,
Stole money, locked up wives, somehow got in:
First away, he led the field and easily won.

It was his simple excellence to be best.
Tough men owned him, their minds beset
By stakes, bookies' doubles, crooked jocks.
He soon became a byword, public asset,
A horse with a nation's soul upon his back—
Australia's Ark of the Covenant, set
Before the people, perfect, loved like God.

And like God to be betrayed by friends.
Sent to America, he died of poisoned food.
In Australia children cried to hear the news
(This Prince of Orange knew no bad or good).
It was, as people knew, a plot of life:
To live in strength, to excel and die too soon,
So they drained his body and they stuffed his skin.

Twenty years later on Sunday afternoons
You still can't see him for the rubbing crowds.
He shares with Bradman and Ned Kelly some
Of the dirty jokes you still can't say out loud.
It is Australian innocence to love
The naturally excessive and be proud
Of a thoroughbred bay gelding who ran fast.

Night Out

Two friends talked of dark politics in light—
Of bombs, catastrophes their lives had found.
Forgotten cars were waiting in the night
To take them to the fiction of their homes and land.

Though two men brimmed with facts all that was said
Spilled like dull wine that overflowed a brink
Of glass, and soon was gone. So each grey head
Did not clear words from smoke and say what he could
    think.

Then one man sought a metaphor, a way
That might unravel knots that held his frown.
The room was deep and wise and heard him say
"The signposts of the world have broken, fallen down."

They nodded, paused. A clock frowned in the smoke
And two men rose to find their hats and coats
As neat as truth. Directionless, they woke
From words to walk through night and seek their starry wits,

The comfort of a gate, a path that rose
Courageously. Each man seemed tall and free.
They had two cars that helped them to revise
All roads and found them safe as far as they could see.

BRUCE DAWE

The City: Midnight

Out of the sighs and breath of each small citizen
Clasped in his neutral bed with eye-lids locked
On the frail Pandora's box of consciousness,

Out of the blind susurrus of limbs
Moving like weeds within sleep's rhythmic waters,
Marked by the metronome of clock and moon,

Out of the shadowy cubes stacked carelessly
On night's blue nursery floor by infant men,
Rises the vast and tremulous O of dreams. . . .

    The knitting spider watches from her shelf,
    The vague and changing shapes of furniture wait;
    Now slippered ghosts grope down familiar stairs,

    While from mysterious doorways, very soon,
    The starlit insomniacs toddle, arms extending
    Headless golliwog, frayed teddy, broken drum.

Down the long streets they go; they will not wake;
They will walk miles before they turn back, weary,
Clutching the dolls they could not give away.

Morning again will prise their fingers loose,
And all their playthings crumble into light.

Only the Beards Are Different

Among the first to go are always a few
Of the strong man's friends, crumpling up
Against the sun-pocked wall, relieved at last
Of the terrible burden of his friendship.
Cruel necessity follows him everywhere.
And the face that was once a dream
Of a patch of baked earth to the landless
And a living wage has lost its inner light,
Faded, and now, deathless and untrue,
Flaps in the memory like a wind-blown poster.
Behind the monolithic smile, the frighteningly
Public eyes, a thousand trigger-fingers tense;
Sadist and pimp resume
Their tricky trades. Caught in two minds,
Men look the other way when truth cries out, that leprous

Mendicant whose importunity must be discouraged.
Travellers find the once-welcoming
Doors closed to them now; over the evening meal
The children are eyed suspiciously, radios
Turned up louder and louder to cover
All the embarrassing noises a revolution makes
In passing—the tumbrils, the firing-squads, the screams
From the underground prison,
The rifle-butts at the door, the conspirators' whisper,
The drums, the marching-songs, the hysterical spiel
Of bandaleroed barkers plugging the ancient wares. . . .

Somewhere the country's saviour cries in his sleep.

CHARLES HIGHAM

Barnacle Geese

Amid the stony slapping of the waves
That break your prow, they cling and shudder; graves
Of light and life that burn in narrow shells.
Stern the trapped wings in glassy architraves,
Where ring for ever the sea's burning bells,
Deeper than sleep, her proud and soundless wells.

Grinds hard the swell. Cold to the hounded hulk
The wolverines, those ravenous tempests skulk
Under the brimming sail; down from the side
The clustering barnacles are rent and shorn
Into the maw of night; downward they glide
Choking the gullet with their iron spawn.

And as they shimmer to the ocean-bed
From each, as each unlocks its trapped-up, dead
Horde of long sleep, long sickness, long despair,
Wings from the winged storm rise, steer to the red

Ramparts of sky as though their hearts were bled,
Feathers like leaves lie scattered everywhere.

March on the sky. Your nets may never catch
Strong cohorts in that dawn, though breezes snatch
Your sheets, and like the Dutchman's phantom heave
Night after night at an eternal latch
The heavens may not loosen, though he grieve
For ever for the death he can't retrieve.

The birds are gone. A day, a night, a day
They linger on beyond the mind's eye; grey
Threads of a scattered banner; tossed and blind,
Their eyes the hollow windows of a tomb.
And should you glimpse them in that sun and wind
You'd almost think them presagers of doom.

Yet see. Night falls again. The breeze
Settles in sheets of foam. The shaking trees
Of islands nod their dreams upon the land.
Wisdom is foundered as the evening flees
Wavering and pale across the skein of sand.
The evening gathers doves. Dark marbles stand

In haunted attitudes of sleep; afar
The wild geese wander backward past the star
And settle round your ships, their great heads bent
In prayer like another firmament
Beneath the mirrored wain; a thousand wings
Burning with wonder as the ocean sings.

Sail on! But sailing keep the soundless rage
Of splendour streaming from each wing, a page
Unsullied in your book. Remember when
Beating the main back, shouting at your men,
That from your side, each crying like a lover,
The wild geese rose, and the storm winds blew over.

EVAN JONES

Noah's Song

The animals are silent in the hold,
Only the lion coughing in the dark
As in my ageing arms once more I fold
My mistress and the mistress of the Ark.

That, the rain, and the lapping of the sea:
Too many years have brought me to this boat
Where days swim by with such monotony,
Days of the fox, the lion and the goat.

Her breathing and the slow beat of the clock
Accentuate the stillness of the room,
Whose walls and floor and ceiling seem to lock
Into a space as single as the tomb.

A single room set up against the night,
The hold of animals, and nothing more;
For any further world is out of sight—
There are no people, and there is no shore.

True, the time passes in unbroken peace:
To some, no doubt, this Ark would seem a haven.
But all that I can hope for is release.
Tomorrow I'll send out the dove and raven.

PHILIP MARTIN

In March

Be mute, this autumn; gather in the world.
And let the soft-trilled cricket speak for you,
Singing in the warm grass or the wakeful night
Beneath late-fallen leaves and the smell of dew.

Gather the world in, gather all its sounds;
And yet, yourself, be silent. Words grow stale,
And with a dull astonishment the heart
Pausing a moment hears its music fail.

O heart, the season's voices call like sleep,
Yet sing you to your waking: even so,
After long winter, people in cold lands catch
The soft clear cry of water under the snow.

CHRISTOPHER KOCH

Half-heard

On the road through the hills I thought I heard it,
Something moving, coming with evening,
In its slow warm breathing through the paddock-land.
The few and spiteful houses there ignored it.

It had come from the coast. I stood on the coast,
Where gulls cried angrily for something that moved,
In the sun-plains across the sea.
The water there was heavy with its hand.

And one by one the evening waves caressed the sullen sand.
Quietly they pondered on nothing at all,
On the laying of their long quiet hands, perhaps,
Upon the waiting beach.

Considering carefully nothing at all,
They too ignored the bird's half-baffled cry.

SYLVIA LAWSON

Trader's Return

Ten years being enough of copra, he souvenired a
whalestooth and came home, not hoping to take
up Sydney where he'd cut its knots and let
them plop in the trawler's wake—
women and all: those parties begun with quiet
Friday beer and abstractions and carried on
through wild fruit-punch and comic-opera riot
to gin and tolerance on Sunday night.

"I mustn't expect," he thought, "I must disconnect.
Though we shuffled all the isms and religions
like cards, took on whichever gods were game,
used history for our private flock of pigeons,
those birds are home to roost, the party's over,
nobody's got the time now to think
in universals, the Social Muse has had it,
nobody's Fabian or even pink.

"The boys are professional blokes on the side of culture,
and every man has a wife to take to bed;
the girls are married—oh, let me disconnect;
it is another city and those girls are dead—
married to artists with Czech or Italian names. . . ."
New neon ads sprang round him like a forest,
and at the corner where the café used to be
stood a T.V. supply shop and a florist's.

But at the place with pink murals he suddenly found them.
Their wives were human. He heard them call him Jack
in their own voices; they made it a party, but in
the middle of an anecdote, he lost track,
seeing that though they'd done it without typhoons
or spray in the face they were older, being in fact
islanders too who of necessity
made disconnectedness a daily act.

VIVIAN SMITH

Bedlam Hills

Corroded flat as hills allow,
stubbled with stones and brittle weeds,
only the thorn blooms here
and scatters its seeds.

The hills are blank and pale now
beneath the clear and static air.
The landscape is as empty
as a blindman's stare.

Mad Clare, the story tells,
gathered her sticks and pieces here.
Her mind wore on the open rock.
But we forget Clare,

walk over and over the hills of strewn
and fractured rock where the berry
suckles the given stone
and the light breaks clearly.

These are the cold, the worn hills
with madness in their monotone
and emptiness where no life moves
beneath a stone.

The Last Summer

The hawk with heavy-lidded eyes
falls through a world of loaded skies,
falls and tears the light with its eye:
falling hawk and falling sky.

Falling, falls, falling dies:
the hawk with drought inside its eyes;

VIVIAN SMITH

fruit falls and splits and dries,
falls with fullness, falls with weight,
the hawk falls alive with hate.
Weight of colour, weight of years:
how can fruit contain its years,
the hawk its tense and nervous hate?
Black and red and blue and gold
falling, fall, cannot withhold.

And like a knife a scarlet bird
sings deserts in the lemon-trees.

The light is torn across with black,
the mountain sings alive with hate;
red and gold and green and black
cathedral trees fall through the air
and burn the earth to love and hate.
O trees burn and purge despair
and crash like churches through the air

while like a knife a scarlet bird
sings deserts in the lemon-trees.

DAVID MALOUF

At My Grandmother's

An afternoon late summer, in a room
shuttered against the bright, envenomed leaves;
an underwater world, where time, like water,
was held in the wide arms of a gilded clock,
and my grandmother, turning in the still sargasso
of memory, wound out her griefs and held
a small boy prisoner to weeds and corals,
while summer leaked its daylight through his head.

I feared that room: the parrot screeching soundless
in its dome of glass, the faded butterflies
like jewels pinned against a sable cloak;
and my grandmother, winding out the skeins I held
like trickling time, between my outstretched arms;

feared most of all the stiff, bejewelled fingers
pinned at her throat or moving on grey wings
from word to word; and feared her voice that called
down from their gilded frames the ghosts of children
who played at hoop and ball, whose spindrift faces
(the drowned might wear such smiles) looked out across
the wrack and debris of the years, to where
a small boy sat, as they once sat, and held
in the wide ache of his arms, all time, like water,
and watched the old grey hands wind out his blood.

CHRIS WALLACE-CRABBE

Love Poem

Written under Capricorn, a land
Two centuries and half a globe away
From pastoral conventions at their end.
The shepherds and the nymphs have had their day
And merciless beauty will no longer make
The stuff of formal poems. So I take
This plainer speech to say what I must say:
Love breaks upon my cold hills like the sun.

I cannot fabricate a green email
To set this gift of love in, so my heart
Must be stripped bare; I cannot spin a tale
Of goddesses in fabled groves apart
Or fob my passions off on bushland swains.

Therefore have patience—take my stumbling pains
In this morass of words as love's report
And glow upon my cold hills like the sun.

All language fails me in the trembling dark,
And I would give my body to you entire
To show a love my poor words cannot mark
The bounds of. Yet, although consumed by fire,
I do not give again this shape of flesh
Which you, already, always hold in mesh;
And so I build these phrases for love's choir.
Love sings upon my cold hills like the sun.

And while our leaning poplar-tree turns bare,
Then green, then bare again above our heads,
We draw love from ourselves and from the air
And learn to weave its casual bright threads
Into a tough and subtle web that can
Outlast our youth and in our twilight span
Be refuge from decay and gathering dreads
While love still warms our cold hills like the sun.

One thing is now assured; should hemispheres,
As well they may, divide us for a space,
Beyond the echoes and the parting tears
Your image in my heart will gather grace
And, like a stretching spring, my love will grow
Ever more taut the farther out I go,
Till all my days are haunted by your face.
Love breaks upon my cold hills like the sun.

Where once was no direction, now there run
These warm and glowing bars of eastern light,
And love breaks on my cold hills like the sun.

Ancient Historian

The drowsy Herodotus holds him there;
He drums his nervous fingers on the page
And glares around the library again
With indignation that is almost rage.
A bookish valour arms him to the teeth;
His abstract love of war and copulation
Is turbine to this blood and, spurning print,
He seethes with all the fire of one ambition:

To lead a narrow band of dead Italians
In through the door past Dr Johnson's bust—
Stout Marius, and Catilina soiling
His well-bred feet in the rebellious dust,
And Clodius encouraging his mob
To cry out "*Panem et circenses!*" here.
Perhaps that might disturb a few thick heads
And blow some dust out of the atmosphere.

Vitality, he muses, is the stair
By which we climb to join the armoured great,
The toll extracted by our family gods,
The virtue proper to both man and state.
But, caught in sudden vision, he recalls
A town once founded on vitality,
Rome, sprawling and gone rotten at the core,
And the lean Goths encroaching silently.

Eyewitness

Don't get the wrong idea;
nothing much unusual occurred.
He started out a normal man—
somewhat better featured

more courageous and ingenious
than any of the others, that was all.
Then, being rather wearied with the sameness
of the company—the lack of novelty—
he merely reproduced himself;
just the sort of sleight of hand

you often see in Middle Eastern places.
That was all. Except that then he turned
a moonstone colour, swelled like dead fish do
in water, rising upside down above us
till so small was he, that I
—for one—could not distinguish him

among the particles of dust around
the sloping sun. There's nothing more to tell
Unless, of course, I mention how the others
martyred his child and afterwards, convinced
that what goes up must then come down,
stood waiting twenty centuries

to do the same to him
as soon as he should reappear.
But nothing much unusual occurred;
don't get the wrong idea.

THOMAS W. SHAPCOTT

Three Kings Came

Three Kings came
with hard gifts of gold
to pay their way
to another world.

THOMAS W. SHAPCOTT

Three Kings came
with bribes of myrrh
to please the gods
and to gain favour.

Three Kings came
with frankincense

and the people saw
their few flung pence
and full of awe
they grovelled deep.

The child himself stayed fast asleep.

The Finches

A tiny spill of bird-things in a swirl
and crest and tide that splashed the garden's edge—
a chatterful of finches filled the hedge
and came upon us with a rush and curl
and scattering of wings. They were so small
I laughed to see them ludicrously gay
among the thorny stalks, and all that day
they teased me with their tiny-throated call.

They were a jest, a scampering of neat
brisk sweets, they were all such frivolities
I did not think to call them real, I was
too merry with their flight to see the heat
that angered their few days, to recognize
my own stern hungers in their fragile cries.

207

JUDITH GREEN

The Bush-fiddle

The bush-fiddle's broken.
A thin pale nylon
note unspoken
curls to silence.

The string unswinging
that fished for death
lives transfixed, singing
its onedrawn breath.

Like a sprouting twig
of the mantleshelf
it hangs by a peg
and sings itself.

Tentatively
the little gourd
dreams its symphony
("The Unheard").

Keats would have liked it.
Keats died young.
But it's not unlikely
he knows the tune.

Calmly it ponders
the cold square hearth
and grows to the roundness
of sky and earth.

Its bush-fruit belly
is fat as the sun
and brown as a gully
and quiet as long.

JUDITH GREEN

The calabash made once
a coolamon
for a black bush baby;
for me a song

a slow ripe fall
of fruit and tendril
so full so still
I cannot mend it.

DON MAYNARD

Athlete

Adam is a pupil of mine
apple of teachers eye

is not a carpenter
or a thinker / still
something of each
and is singularly attracted to
sprinting & hurdling

squatters son Adam likes
the land when it is fresh & green
oranges with navels
& to be seen in the lithe grass

would surely pass
any old lovemaking test you like

set to sprint the hundred
he feels the future pause with him
then break into the wide skin
as he strides the wind

his early experience the songs of birds
every season of the year
& me yelling at him
I say '*poise* Adam is to be
desired' say to him drawn back
like an arrow on a bow

GEOFFREY LEHMANN

The Last Campaign

In the hot valley of the never was
This crumbling army stands, dry, mummified,
The cornet raising to his lips the horn
That never sounded, and a thousand hands
Clenching the hilts of swords they never raised,
Ranks of dead cavalry staring into nothing.

Strong liquor, songs shouted around the campfire
And excellent weather marked the setting out
Of this campaign against the powers of darkness,
And men from every village that they passed
Came out to join their ranks. For many weeks
They journeyed, for long months in fact across
The sunlit plateau and began to curse
The cloudless weather and demand a battle,
And every time they saw pale smoke at dusk
Rise from behind a hill, the veterans sniffed
With pleasure, stared hard through the twilight haze
And rode around the bend with sabres ready,
But always men in their own uniform
Rode out to join them.
                              So this cavalcade
Rode finally into the fatal valley,
Saw from the other end approaching them

A distant cloud of dust, sparkling with points,
(Was it the gleam of weapons?) and discerned
A barley audible thunder (Was it hooves?)
And headlong rode towards the cloud of dust
Which spread out and became a vast concourse
Of horsemen spurring sweating horses on.
Headlong they rode against the enemy,
Then saw they charged an image of themselves,
A mere reflection in an airy mirror—
And men, plumes, horses, suddenly all froze.

And so this army still stands in the valley,
The gold braid and black ostrich feathers crumbling
Of riders who still hold the fraying reins
Of horses with their hooves raised in mid air.

RANDOLPH STOW

The Utopia of Lord Mayor Howard

> "Lord Mayor Howard . . . said that the
> trees on the corner had grown so
> tall that they had lost their
> attraction. Neat rose gardens
> would be much more attractive."—
> *The West Australian.*

His delicate fingers, moving among the roses,
became a symbol. His words, a battle-cry.
"Nothing shall be taller than Lord Mayor Howard
but insurance buildings."

A fanatical army, wild with Cromwellian zeal,
laid waste Kings Park, denuded Darlington.
Guerillas of Pemberton fried alive in their forests,

as mile on mile, that the giant unattractive karri
had once encumbered, fell thrall to triumphant Peace.

And not Peace alone, but also Dame Edith Helen,
Comtesse Vandal, and even a brand new strain:
Mrs Lord Mayor Howard.

Only you and I, my subversive and admirable brethren,
did not join in the celebrations. A malicious rumour
that some of us had been seen to spit on roses
obliged us to fly the land.

On Kerguelen, New Amsterdam, and such friendly islands
pitching our tents, and on each one planting one karri,
under the name of Yggdrasil we worshipped them.
—Tenderly, humbly, as became the last plants on earth
that were taller than Lord Mayor Howard.

And although the news of our ruthless persecution
of every breed of rose caused shudders in Guildford,
and although our faith, known as anti-Rosaceanism,
was condemned in the United Nations and *The Times*,

the remembrance of our trees so sighs in their sleep
that the immigrants have been more than we can handle.
And in truth, we half expect to see Lord Mayor Howard.

Dust

"Enough," she said. But the dust still rained around her;
over her living-room (hideous, autumnal)
dropping its small defiance.
                              The clock turned green.
She spurned her broom and took a train. The neighbours
have heard nothing.

Jungles, deserts, stars—the six days of creation—
came floating in, gold on a chute of light.
In May, grudging farmers admired the carpet
and foretold a rich year.

Miraculous August! What shelves of yellow capeweed,
what pouffes of everlastings. We worship nature
in my country.

Never such heath as flowered on the virgin slopes
of the terrible armchairs. Never convolvulus
brighter than that which choked the china dogs.
Bushwalkers' Clubs boiled their billies with humility
in chimneys where orchids and treesnakes
luxuriantly intertwined.

A photographer came from *The West Australian*, and ten
teenage reportresses. Teachers of botany
overflowed to the garden.

Indeed, trains were run from Yalgoo and Oodnadatta.
But the neighbours slept behind sealed doors, with feather
dusters beside their beds.

Ruins of the City of Hay

The wind has scattered my city to the sheep.
Capeweed and lovely lupins choke the street
where the wind wanders in great gaunt chimneys of hay
and straws cry out like keyholes.

Our yellow Petra of the fields: alas!
I walk the ruins of forum and capitol,
through quiet squares, by the temples of tranquillity.
Wisps of the metropolis brush my hair.
I become invisible in tears.
This was no ratbags' Eden: these were true haystacks.
Golden, but functional, our mansions sprang from dreams

of architects in love (*O my meadow queen!*)
No need for fires to be lit on the yellow hearthstones;
our walls were warmer than flesh, more sure than igloos.
On winter nights we squatted naked as Esquimaux,
chanting our sagas of innocent chauvinism.

In the street no vehicle passed. No telephone,
doorbell or till was heard in the canyons of hay.
No stir, no sound, but the sickle and the loom,
and the comments of emus begging by kitchen doors
in the moonlike silence of morning.

Though the neighbour states (said Lao Tse) lie in sight of
     the city
and their cocks wake and their watchdogs warn the inhabi-
     tants
the men of the city of hay will never go there
all the days of their lives.

But the wind of the world descended on lovely Petra
and the spires of the towers and the statues and belfries fell.
The bones of my brothers broke in the breaking columns.
The bones of my sisters, clasping their broken children,
cracked on the hearthstones, under the rooftrees of hay.
I alone mourn in the temples, by broken altars
bowered in black nightshade and mauve salvation-jane.

And the cocks of the neighbour nations scratch in the straw.
And their dogs rejoice in the bones of all my brethren.

Strange Fruit

Suicide of the night—ah, flotsam:
                              (the great
poised thunderous breaker of darkness rearing above you,
and your bones awash, in the shallows, glimmering, stony,
like gods of forgotten tribes, in forgotten deserts)

take care. Take care. For your campfire falters, and firelight
folds, and will clamp around you its charcoal calyx,
and already for many hours your eyes (my terror)
have drowned in deep waters of dream, till I grow fearless.

(Embers of crocodiles love you from the mangroves.
Dingo ears yearn, yearn towards your tranquil breathing.)

Day and the firelight guard you from harm so darkly
rehearsed, removing me far; for by day I dread you,
fearing your quester's ear, that might interpret
what sings in my blood; your eye, that might guess my fever.

But so long as the harsh light lasts, I stalk your horses'
desolate spoor: a statue among the anthills,
should you look back; and prowling—and yearning, yearn-
    ing,
howl out my grief and grievance, and burn in fever.

(Embers of crocodiles love you from the mangroves.
Dingo ears suck the wind for your tranquil breathing.)

I am the country's station; all else is fever.
Did we ride knee to knee down the canyons, or did I dream
    it?
They were lilies of dream we swam in, parrots of myth
we named for each other, "since no one has ever named
    them . . ."

Alone for an hour, in a thicket, I reached for strange fruit.

Now you sleep by the fire. And these are my true eyes
that glare from the swamps. And the rattling howl in the
    gullies
is my true voice. That cries: *You shall try strange fruit.*

215

INDEX OF AUTHORS

with biographical notes

ALLAN, James Alexander. Born in Melbourne in 1889, and educated at Scotch College and Melbourne University. He was in the Commonwealth Public Service from 1912 to 1918 and again from 1942 to 1950; from 1919 to 1939 he was in business. He served with the A.I.F. in Palestine and Africa in World War II. Interested in historical research. Besides prose works, mainly historical, he has published two books of verse: *A Wineshop Madonna* (1911), and *Revolution* (1940).

pp.—25-27

ANDERSON, Ethel; 1883-1958. Born at Leamington, Warwickshire, and educated at the Sydney Church of England Girls' Grammar School. Her parents were Australian, and she spent most of her childhood at Rangamatty, near Picton, N.S.W., the scene of many of her poems. She married Brigadier-General Austin Anderson and lived for some years on the Indian frontier, returning to Australia in 1924. Publications include: *Squatter's Luck* (1942), *Sunday at Yarralumla* (1947), and *The Song of Hagar* (1957). She also wrote essays and short-stories. The poem "Waking Child While You Slept" from the "bucolic eclogues" in *Squatter's Luck* is here printed in a shortened version.

pp.—22-25

ASTLEY, Thea. Born in Brisbane in 1925, and educated at Queensland University where she took a degree in Arts. She has since been teaching with the Education Departments of Queensland and New South Wales. Her publications include poems, short-stories and three novels. In 1960 she was awarded a Commonwealth Literary Fellowship to write a novel of urban life and produced *The Well Dressed Explorer* which subsequently won the Miles Franklin Award in 1963. She is married and has one son.

pp.—176-177

AUCHTERLONIE, Dorothy (Mrs H. M. Green). Born at Sunderland, Durham, England, and educated in England and at North Sydney High School and the University of Sydney, where she took her M.A. She taught at various schools for eight years and was co-principal of Presbyterian Girls' College, Warwick, Queensland. Appointed first woman lecturer at Monash University, 1961. She has two children. Publications: *Kaleidoscope* (1940); and, in collaboration with H. M. Green, the revised edition of *Fourteen Minutes*, criticism (1950).

p.—155

AUSTIN, Albert Gordon. Born in 1918, and educated at Coburg and Melbourne High Schools and University of Melbourne (B.A. 1947, B.Ed. 1952, M.Ed. 1956). Served with A.I.F. in Middle East, New Guinea, 1940-45; M.C. at Alamein, 1942; discharged with rank of Captain, October, 1945. "Thin poetic vein developed during war petered out with horrors of peace." Now married with two daughters, and Senior Lecturer in Education, University of Melbourne. Publications include: *George William Rusden* (1958), *Australian Education, 1788-1900* (1961), *Select Documents in Australian Education, 1788-1900* (1963).

pp.—109-110

BANNING, Lex. Born in Sydney in 1921, and graduated in Arts at Sydney University. He has written for films and radio, has done freelance journalism and book-reviewing, and has been Librarian at the Spastic Centre, Mosman, Sydney. Publications: *Everyman His Own Hamlet* (1951), *The Instant's Clarity* (1952), and *Apocalypse in Springtime* (1956).

pp.—156-157

217

BARRATT, Ken. Born at Christchurch, New Zealand, in 1906, and educated at The Scots College, Sydney. He became assistant editor of the post World War I *Aussie* magazine. Later went into advertising and publicity. Joined Broadcasting Station 2GB and is now Programme Manager. He has contributed to many journals but has never published a book. "Burke and Wills" is his most anthologized piece, but is only one of a longer sequence called "The Explorers". He translated Meyerling for radio and edited *Songs of the Plain* by his uncle Francis H. Brown.

pp.—48-49

BEAVER, Bruce. Born at Manly, N.S.W., in 1928, and educated at Manly public school and Sydney Boys' High School. He has since worked as cow-cocky, radio programme arranger, wages clerk, surveyor's labourer, fruit-picker, proof-reader and occasional journalist. Spent the years 1958-62 mainly in Auckland and Nelson, New Zealand, with a six months' stay on Norfolk Island in 1959. In 1962 he published at his own expense a first book of poems entitled *Under the Bridge*.

p.—190

BIGGS, Maurice. Born at Kadina, S.A., in 1915. He was educated at various private and State schools and finally at Pulteney Grammar School, Adelaide. He attended courses at Adelaide University for a couple of years, and then took to a life of wandering in many parts of the world. He served with the Second A.I.F. in the Middle East, Greece, Crete and Syria, and later in New Guinea, where he was so severely incapacitated that his life was despaired of. He is manager of a Sydney retail store. Publications: *Poems of War and Peace* (1945).

pp.—110-111

BLADEN, Peter. Born in Perth, W.A., in 1922, and graduated M.A. at Melbourne University. His love of Australia has led to a "slightly nomadic" way of life. He has lived in Perth, in Darwin during the war years, Melbourne, and in Queensland, where he

218

owns an island. Publications include: *The Old Ladies at Newington* (1953) and *Masque for a Modern Minstrel* (1962).

pp.—163-165

BLIGHT, John. Born at Unley, South Australia, in 1913. He had high school education, and subsequently qualified as an accountant. He has been a citrus farmer, public accountant, public servant, and at present is a partner in a sawmilling business. He was appointed by the Queensland Government as a Commissioner on the Timber Inquiry Commission 1949-1950. Publications: *The Old Pianist* (1945), *The Two Suns Met* (1954), *A Beachcomber's Diary* (1964).

pp.—89-91

BUCKLEY, Vincent. Born in Victoria in 1925, and educated at St Patrick's College, Melbourne, and the Universities of Melbourne and Cambridge. He has published two books of poetry and two of criticism, as well as many smaller publications. He is on the editorial board of the Catholic review *Prospect*. He is Reader in English at the University of Melbourne.

pp.—177-179

CAMPBELL, David. Born at Ellerslie, Adelong, N.S.W., in 1915, and educated at The King's School, Parramatta, and at Cambridge where he graduated in Arts and played football for England against Ireland and Wales. During the second world war he was a pilot in the R.A.A.F., commanded at different times No.'s 1 and 2 Squadrons and was awarded the D.F.C. and bar. He is married with three children and farms a property near Bungendore, N.S.W. Publications: *Speak With The Sun* (1949), *The Miracle of Mullion Hill* (1956), *Poems* (1962); and *Evening Under Lamplight*, short-stories (1959).

pp.—111-115

CATO, Nancy. Born in Adelaide, South Australia, in 1917, and educated at Presbyterian Girls' College and Adelaide University.

She studied for a short time at S.A. School of Arts. Poet, short-story writer and novelist, edited *Jindyworobak Anthology* (1950), *Southern Festival* (1959), and was for a time advisory editor of *Poetry* (Australia) and *Overland*. Has been journalist, grape-picker, art-critic, and travelled in Europe, Russia, Asia, and the Australian outback. Married, with three children. Chief publications: Novels: *All the Rivers Run, Time Flow Softly, But Still the Stream*, and *Green Grows the Vine*; Verse: *The Darkened Window* (1950), *The Dancing Bough* (1957).

pp.—133-134

CLARK, Robert. Born in Darjeeling, India, in 1911, of Australian parents. He came to South Australia as a boy and is now a lawyer in Adelaide. He was a co-editor of the anthology *Verse in Australia*. Publications: *The Dogman* (1962).

pp.—78-79

COLLINSON, Laurence. Born at Leeds, England, in 1925, but has lived in New Zealand and in various part of Australia since early childhood. His education was erratic except for a longish period at Brisbane State High School. He is at present attached to the Publications Branch of the Victorian Education Department. Publications: *The Moods of Love* (1957), *Who Is Wheeling Grandma?* (1964). Several of his plays—for stage, television, and radio—have been produced.

p.—180

CRAIG, Alexander. Born in 1923, and studied at the University of Melbourne, later doing post-graduate work and teaching—mainly at the University of Iowa—in the U.S.A. He served in New Guinea with the A.I.F. Publications: *Far-back Country* (1954) and *The Living Sky* (1964).

pp.—167-169

DAVIS, Norma L., 1905-1945. Born at Whitemore, near West-bury, Tasmania, and educated at State school. Suffering many years of ill-health, she lived quietly at Perth, Tasmania, and wrote of the countryside around her. Her best poems were collected in *Earth Cry* (1943).

pp.—46-47

DAWE, Bruce. Born at Geelong, Vic., in 1930. He left Northcote High School at sixteen and worked as farmhand, mill-hand, copy-boy, gardener and postman. In 1954 he began an Arts course at Melbourne University. Became a Catholic in the same year. He is now in the R.A.A.F. Publications: *No Fixed Address* (1962).

pp.—194-196

DOBSON, Rosemary de Brissac. Born in Sydney in 1920, and educated at Frensham and Sydney University. She has studied art, and has worked as a member of the editorial staff of Angus and Robertson. She is married to A. T. Bolton, editor of Ure Smith Pty Ltd. Publications: *In a Convex Mirror* (1944), *The Ship of Ice* (1948), *Child With A Cockatoo* (1955). Another book of poems is in preparation.

pp.—143-147

DUNN, Max. Born in Dublin in 1895, and educated at Winchester, the Sorbonne, Edinburgh and Columbia Universities. After practising as a psychotherapist for some years, he became a professional writer. Of his thirty published books, the following are volumes of poems: *Stardust and Clay, Mirror to Mind, Random Elements, No Asterisks, Time of Arrival, Portrait of a Country, The Journey of John Donne, The Journey of Diornos, The Mirror and the Rose, Into the Radiance,* and *Leaves of Jade* (a series of poems translated from the Chinese).

p.—32

DUTTON, Geoffrey. Born at Anlaby, South Australia, in 1922, and educated at Geelong Grammar School and Oxford. In World War II he was a flight-lieutenant with the R.A.A.F. He

R

has travelled extensively in Europe, the Middle East, and America. Besides a novel, *The Mortal and the Marble* (1950), he has written short-stories, travel books, biography and art criticism. His publications in verse are: *Night-Flight and Sunrise* (1944), *Antipodes in Shoes* (1958), *Flowers and Fury* (1962).

pp.—166-167

FAIRBRIDGE, W. S., 1918-1950. Born at Perth, W.A., and educated at Christ's Hospital, the Bluecoat School, in Sussex. He was a son of Kingsley Fairbridge, the South African Rhodes Scholar and founder of the Fairbridge Farm Schools. He returned to Australia to graduate in science at the University of Western Australia, afterwards specializing in marine biology with the C.S.I.R.O. He died from poliomyelitis. His *Collected Poems* was published posthumously in 1953.

pp.—139-142

FINNIN, Mary (Mrs. J. J. Connellan). Born at Geelong and educated at Geelong and Melbourne University. She has studied and travelled extensively in Europe and has worked at teaching, industrial relations research and Australian historical research. She is an artist as well as a writer and has held successful exhibitions. Interested in fishing and gardening. Publications: *A Beggar's Opera* (1938), *Look Down, Olympians* (1939), *Royal* (1941), *Alms for Oblivion* (1947), *The Shield of Place* (1957).

pp.—79-80

FrrzGERALD, Robert David. Born at Hunter's Hill, Sydney, in 1902, and educated at Sydney Grammar School and Sydney University. His grandfather was Deputy Surveyor-General for New South Wales and an authority on Australian orchids. Fitz-Gerald qualified as a land surveyor in 1925 and spent some years in Fiji where many of his poems are located. He is now a senior surveyor in the Commonwealth Department of the Interior. He was awarded the O.B.E. for services to literature in 1951. Publications: *The Greater Apollo* (1927), *To Meet the Sun*

(1929), *Moonlight Acre* (1938), *Between Two Tides* (1952), *This Night's Orbit* (1953), *Southmost Twelve* (1963), *The Elements of Poetry*, criticism (1963).

pp.—36-44

GRANO, Paul Langton. Born at Ararat, Vic., in 1894, and educated at St Patrick's College, Ballarat: LL.B., Melbourne University. After a few years' legal practice he followed various occupations, and finally settled in Brisbane, where he joined the Public Service and is now retired. Founded Catholic Poetry Society (Bris.) 1934 and, after the war, Catholic Writers' and Readers' Society (1943). One of the four original contributors to *Meanjin Papers*. Publications: *The Roads and Other Poems* (1934), *Quest* (1940), *Poet's Holiday* (1941), *Poems New and Old* (1945).

pp.—30-32

GREEN, Judith. Born at Perth, W.A., in 1936 and educated at Brisbane Girls' Grammar School and the universities of Queensland and Cambridge. She taught for a year at Fairholme Girls' College, Toowoomba, and has lectured in English at the University of Queensland. Her poems are included in *Four Poets* (1962).

pp.—208-209

HALL, Rodney. Born at Solihull, Warwickshire, in 1935. After school in England and Australia, he started work at the age of sixteen. In 1958 he travelled overseas, visiting most European countries and taking whatever jobs he could find. At present he is an actor and scriptwriter for radio and TV. In his spare time he plays the clarinet. He lives in Brisbane with his wife and daughter. Publications: *Penniless till Doomsday* (1962), *Statues and Lovers* (in *Four Poets*, 1962); and *Forty Beads on a Hangman's Rope* (1963).

pp.—205-206

HARRIS, Max. Born in Adelaide in 1921, and educated at St Peter's College and the University of Adelaide. He founded the publishing firm of Reed and Harris, and in the early 1940s was the editor of the *avant garde* magazine *Angry Penguins*. He is co-editor with Geoffrey Dutton of the quarterly *Australian Letters* and is well-known as a critic on radio, TV, and in various magazines. He has published a novel, *The Vegetative Eye*, and three books of verse, of which the most recent is *The Coorong* (1955).

pp.—157-160

HART-SMITH, William. Born at Tunbridge Wells, England, in 1911. He had a year's schooling in Scotland and another two in England before going to New Zealand at the age of twelve. He started work in New Zealand at fifteen, and came to Australia in 1936. In Australia he was a copy-writer and announcer with 2CH, and then became Air Publicity Officer with the A.B.C., Sydney, until enlistment with the A.I.F. late in 1940. After the war he lived in Darwin and Sydney, then spent some years in New Zealand, returning to Sydney in 1962. Publications: *Columbus Goes West* (1943), *Harvest* (1945), *The Unceasing Ground* (1946), *Christopher Columbus* (1948), *On the Level* (1950), *Poems of Discovery* (1959).

pp.—80-83

HARWOOD, Gwen. Born in Brisbane in 1920, and educated at the Brisbane Girls' Grammar School. After leaving school she continued to study music, taught music, and was organist at All Saints' Church, Brisbane. She has lived in Tasmania since 1945, and is married, with four children. Her first book, *Poems*, was published in 1963.

pp.—147-152

HEALY, Ian. Born in Newcastle, N.S.W., in 1919. He was educated in Newcastle and worked for some years as an announcer-scriptwriter at commercial radio stations. After serving in the second A.I.F. as a sergeant, he joined the journalistic staff of the *Newcastle Morning Herald* in 1945. He left this newspaper in 1954, spent two years free-lancing abroad, rejoined the *Herald* in 1956 and was its daily columnist and theatre critic till resigning in 1963 to join the Department of the Interior News and Information Bureau in Canberra. His poems have appeared in magazines and anthologies.

p.—142

HIGHAM, Charles. Born in London in 1931, and educated privately. He worked as a bookseller and publisher's assistant (1951-56); was a book critic for the *Sydney Morning Herald* (1956-62); and is at present literary editor of the *Bulletin*. Publications include: *A Distant Star* (1951), *Spring and Death* (1953), *The Earthbound and Other Poems* (1959).

pp.—196-197

HOPE, Alec Derwent. Born at Cooma, N.S.W., in 1907. He was educated at Lesley House School, Hobart, and at Bathurst and Fort Street High Schools; took B.A. degrees at the University of Sydney and the University of Oxford, and entered the N.S.W. Department of Education in 1932. In 1938 he became a lecturer at the Sydney Teachers' College and was subsequently Senior Lecturer in the University of Melbourne, and is now Professor of English at the Australian National University. He has published two books of poems, *The Wandering Islands* (1955) and *Poems* (1960).

pp.—52-63

HOPEGOOD, Peter. Born near Billericay, Essex, in 1891, and educated at Dover College, Aspatria Agricultural College, and Brighton Municipal Art School. From 1910 to 1914 he visited Saskatchewan and Alberta, Canada. Served with Essex Regiment, 1914-1918. Awarded MC and bar. He came to Perth in 1924. Publications: *Austral Pan* (1932), *Thirteen from Oahu* (1940), *Circus at World's End* (1947), *Snake's-eye View of a Serial Story* (1964), and autobiography *Peter Lecky, by himself* (1935).

pp.—28-30

HUDSON, Flexmore. Born at Charters Towers in 1913, and educated at various schools in New Zealand, N.S.W. and Adelaide, and at Adelaide University. Was head-teacher in country schools for twelve years. Then he took a variety of jobs, including seaman on a schooner and freelance writer. Has been Senior Master of English at Scotch College, Adelaide, for thirteen years and till recently Rowing Master and coach of the Eights. Author of seven books of verse, the last two being *As Iron Hills* (1944) and *Pools of the Cinnabar Range* (1960); also *The Child Discovers Poetry*, aesthetics; *Discovery*, a children's book; and various stories in periodicals and anthologies. Published and edited *Poetry*, the International Quarterly of Verse (1940-1947).

p.—91

INGAMELLS, Rex, 1913-1955. Born at Orraroo, South Australia, and educated at Prince Alfred College and the University of Adelaide. He was a high school teacher with the South Australian Education Department, subsequently joining the staff of the publishing firm of Georgian House, Melbourne. He was the founder of the Jindyworobak movement and editor of many of its publications. He was killed in a motor accident. A selection from his seven preceding books of verse was published in *Selected Poems* (1944); his long poem *The Great South Land* was published in 1951.

PP.—92-93

IRVIN, Eric. Born in 1908 and educated in Sydney. He enlisted in the Army in May 1940, and served in the Libyan, Syrian, New Guinea (twice) and Borneo campaigns with the 7th Division. On discharge in 1945 he entered journalism, and is now on the editorial staff of the *Sydney Morning Herald*. His poems were published in *A Soldier's Miscellany* (1945).

PP.—73-74

IRVIN, Margaret. Born in 1916, and educated at Holy Cross College, Woollahra. Her verse has been published in magazines and anthologies. She is the wife of Eric Irvin and mother of three children.

pp.—128-129

JONES, Evan. Born in Melbourne in 1931, and educated at Melbourne High School and the University of Melbourne. From teaching history at that University, he went in 1958 to Stanford University (California) on a Writing Scholarship. In 1960 he returned to a lectureship in English at the Australian National University. Publications: *Inside the Whale* (1960).

p.—198

KEESING, Nancy. Born in Sydney in 1923, and educated at Sydney Church of England Girls' Grammar School and Frensham. Diploma of Social Studies from Sydney University. Worked as a clerk for the Department of the Navy during the war; as a trained social worker and as a freelance writer. Married A. M. Hertzberg. Publications: *Imminent Summer* (1951), *Three Men and Sydney* (1955), *By Gravel and Gum*, for children (1963). Edited (in collaboration with Douglas Stewart) *Australian Bush Ballads* (1955), *Old Bush Songs* (1957).

pp.—169-172

KOCH, Christopher. Born in Hobart, Tasmania, in 1932. His great-great-grandfather was a German architect who migrated to Victoria from Hamburg. Koch was educated at St Virgil's College and Hobart State High School, and graduated in Arts at the University of Tasmania. He went abroad at the age of twenty-two, and worked for two years at various jobs in London. From 1957 until 1959 he worked for the A.B.C. as a Schools Broadcasts producer in Sydney. In 1960 he went abroad again, spending a year in the U.S.A., and a year in Milan, Italy, where he taught English. He has now returned to the A.B.C. and is at present with Schools Broadcasts in Melbourne. He is married, with one son. In 1958 he published a novel, *The Boys in the Island*.

p.—199

LANGLEY, Eve. Born at Forbes, N.S.W., in 1908. She was edu-
cated at various schools, and afterwards worked on the land in
Gippsland, Victoria. She went to New Zealand in 1932, where
her prize-winning novel *The Pea Pickers* was written. Subse-
quently she returned to Australia where a second novel, *White
Topee* (1954) was published. She lives in the Blue Mountains in
New South Wales. Her poems have appeared in magazines and
anthologies.

pp.—74-75

LAWSON, Sylvia. Born in Sydney in 1932, and educated at Fort
Street Girls' High School and the University of Sydney. Has
worked for Sydney daily newspapers, the Sydney Film Festival,
and the independent fortnightly *Nation*. Married in 1955 to
Keith Thomas; has two sons. She has published verse, articles,
criticism of books and films; and is currently working on a bio-
graphical study of J. F. Archibald.

p.—200

LEHMANN, Geoffrey. Born in Sydney in 1940, and educated at
Shore School, Sydney. He has completed an Arts-Law course and
is at present working as a solicitor. He has co-edited the univer-
sity magazines *Arna* and *Hermes*. His output includes some long
poems, chiefly unpublished, about flowers, cats and biblical sub-
jects. He has won the Poetry Society of Australia's £50 award
and has been published in various overseas and Australian
anthologies and magazines.

pp.—210-211

LLYWELYN. Of pioneer stock, Beryl Llywelyn Lucas was born
at Harkaway, Vic., in the foothills of the Dandenongs. She uses
the middle name which commemorates her father, the Rev. Ab.
Llywelyn Lucas, who died young, before she was born. Her
mother was a pioneer in the qualified-nursing profession—Mary
Janet MacKie. She was educated at Presbyterian Ladies College
(N.S.W. and Vic.) and night University classes Melbourne, also

228

London. Graduated School of Horticulture, Burnley, Vic., and earned her living in horticulture and free-lancing. Contributed *Triad, Bulletin, Stead's English Poetry*, etc. She has published two books of verse, *The Garden* (1938) and *On Wings* (1944).

pp.—47-48

MACAINSH, Noel. Born at Horsham, Vic., in 1926. He attended various country schools, served with the R.A.A.F., then practised as a chartered engineer. Subsequently he engaged on literary research, under a Commonwealth Award, in the Department of Germanic Languages at the University of Melbourne. His poetry has appeared in anthologies and magazines. He is also the author of critical articles, translations and a book on art.

p.—189

McAULEY, James. Born at Lakemba, N.S.W., in 1917, and educated at Fort Street High School and Sydney University. After service in the Australian Army Directorate of Research and Civil Affairs during the war, he became lecturer in Government at the Australian School of Pacific Administration. He visited New Guinea frequently and wrote articles on New Guinea affairs. In 1956 he became editor of *Quadrant*. In 1961 he accepted an invitation to become Reader in Poetry at the University of Tasmania, and subsequently was appointed Professor of English. Publications: *Under Aldebaran* (1946), *A Vision of Ceremony* (1956), *The End of Modernity*, essays (1959), *Captain Quiros* (1964).

pp.—134-138

McDONALD, Nan. Born at Eastwood, N.S.W., in 1921, and educated at Hornsby Girls' High School and the University of Sydney. Publications: *Pacific Sea* (1947), *The Lonely Fire* (1954), *The Lighthouse* (1959).

pp.—160-163

McKELLAR, J. A. R., 1904-1932. Born at Dulwich Hill, Sydney, and educated at Sydney High School. He joined the staff of the Bank of New South Wales, where his career was exceptionally promising until cut short by his untimely death from pneumonia after a game of first-grade Rugby football. He was outstanding at many sports and was a keen student of English, French, Greek and Roman literature. The poem by which he is represented in this anthology is part of a sequence, "Fourth Napoleon", which in his posthumous *Collected Poems* (1946) is described as "incomplete and unrevised".

pp.—45-46

MACKENZIE, Kenneth, 1913-1955. Born at Perth, W.A., and educated at Guildford Grammar School, Muresk Agricultural College, and the University of Western Australia. He came to Sydney in 1934 and worked as film and dramatic critic for *Smith's Weekly* and other newspapers. Before he was drowned at Goulburn, N.S.W., he had been working on the land at Kurrajong in the Blue Mountains. He wrote several novels under the name of Seaforth Mackenzie, of which the best-known is *The Young Desire It* (1937), reprinted in Sirius Books (1963). His books of verse are: *Our Earth* (1937), *The Moonlit Doorway* (1944), *Selected Poems* (1961).

pp.—93-102

McCUAIG, Ronald. Born in Newcastle, N.S.W., in 1908, and went to school at Mayfield and Killara. Intended for softgoods warehousing, he deviated into radio journalism (*Wireless Weekly*), went round the world in 1939, returned to radio journalism (*A.B.C. Weekly*); then *Smith's Weekly*, the *Sydney Morning Herald* and twelve years on the literary staff of the *Bulletin*. Since 1961 he has been on the staff of the Australian Commonwealth News and Information Bureau, Canberra. His books of verse *Vaudeville* (1938), *The Wanton Goldfish* (1941), and *Quod Ronald McCuaig* (1946) were included with additional poems in *The Ballad of Bloodthirsty Bessie and Other Poems*

(1961). Some essays and short-stories, *Tales Out of Bed*, were published in 1944. He married in 1934 and has two sons.

pp.—67-72

MALOUF, David. Born in Brisbane in 1934. A graduate of the University of Queensland, he was for some time a lecturer in the Department of English there. In 1959 he left Australia to spend some years in England and Europe. His poems are included in *Four Poets* (1962).

pp.—202-203

MANIFOLD, John Streeter. Born in Melbourne in 1915. He spent his childhood on the family station in S.W. Vic., and was educated at Geelong Grammar and Jesus College, Cambridge. He served in the British Army 1940-46 in England, West Africa, Normandy, Belgium, Holland and Germany. He returned to Australia in 1949 and now lives with his English wife and two children at Wynnum, not far out of Brisbane. Publications: two volumes of verse (of which the latest, 1961, is *Nightmares and Sunhorses*), two books on musical subjects, countless articles on musical subjects and folklore, many uncollected short-stories, radio-scripts, and translations from French, German and Chinese poets.

pp.—115-118

MARTIN, David. Born in Budapest in 1915. He received his education in Germany and wrote his first verse in German, published just before and during the second world war. He has lived and worked in Holland, Palestine, Britain and India, and during the Spanish Civil War was in the Medical Corps on the Republican side. Settled in Australia in 1949. He has held many journalistic appointments, particularly in England, and now works as a correspondent for overseas newspapers in Australia. His other professional interest is social research. Principal publications: *Battlefields and Girls*, poems (1942), *The Shepherd and the Hunter*, play (1946), *Tiger Bay*, novel (1946), *The Shoes Men*

231

Walk In, stories (1947), *The Stones of Bombay,* novel (1949), *From Life,* poems (1953), *Poems 1938-1958* (1958), *Spiegel the Cat,* story-poem (1961), *The Young Wife,* novel (1962).

MARTIN, Philip. Born in Melbourne in 1931, and educated at Xavier College and at the University of Melbourne, where he taught in the English Department 1960-62. Now lecturing in English at the Australian National University. Poems in *Australian Poetry,* and in *Melbourne University Magazine* and other University journals.

MATHEW, Ray. Born in Sydney in 1929, and educated at Sydney Boys' High School and Sydney Teachers' College. He taught for three years in small schools in central New South Wales. Since he left teaching in 1952 he has had a variety of jobs—clerk, lecturer, barman, reviewer. Publications: *With Cypress Pine,* verse (1951), *Song and Dance,* verse (1956), *South of the Equator,* verse (1961), *A Bohemian Affair,* stories (1961), *A Spring Song,* play (1961), *Miles Franklin,* criticism (1963).

MATTHEWS, Harley. Born at Fairfield, N.S.W., in 1889, and educated at Sydney High School. After working as a solicitor's clerk he enlisted in the A.I.F. in World War I, and was at Gallipoli. In 1922 he established a vineyard at Moorebank on George's River, N.S.W. Publications include *Under the Open Sky* (1912), *Vintage* (1938), and *The Breaking of the Drought* (1940).

MAURICE, Furnley (F. L. Wilmot); 1881-1942. Born in Melbourne and educated at State schools. As a boy he worked in the bookselling business of E. W. Cole and eventually became manager. In 1932 he became manager of Melbourne University Press.

In 1934 his "Melbourne and Memory" won the poetry competition connected with the Melbourne centenary celebrations. He published many books of verse, among which were *To God: From the Weary Nations* (1917), *The Gully* (1929), *Melbourne Odes* (1934) and (posthumously) *Poems by Furnley Maurice* (1944). The poem "The Victoria Markets Recollected in Tranquillity" is printed in a slightly shortened version in the present anthology.

pp.—14-19

MAYNARD, Don. Born at Rockhampton in 1937. He graduated at the University of Queensland and spent a year as a resident master at Geelong Grammar School, afterwards joining the editorial staff of a Melbourne publisher. His poems are included in *Four Poets* (1962).

pp.—209-210

MOLL, Ernest G. Born at Murtoa, Vic., in 1900, and attended school at Gerogery West, N.S.W., and Concordia College, Adelaide. Received B.A. from Lawrence College, Wisconsin, and M.A. Harvard University. Elected to membership in Phi Beta Kappa. Since 1928 Professor of English in the University of Oregon. He is married, with two children, and retains his Australian citizenship. His books of verse include *Sedge Fire* (1927); *Native Moments* (1931); *Cut from Mulga* (1940); *Brief Waters* (1945); *Beware the Cuckoo* (1947); *The Waterhole* (1948); *The Lifted Spear* (1953); *Poems 1940-55* (1957); *The Rainbow Serpent* (1962).

pp.—32-33

MOORE, T. Inglis. Born at Camden, N.S.W., in 1901, and educated at Sydney Grammar School and St Paul's College, University of Sydney. He graduated B.A. in 1924, and won a travelling scholarship to the University of Oxford, taking his B.A. and M.A. there. He taught English in the United States for two years and as Associate Professor at the University of the Philippines 1927-

233

s

30. On his return to Australia in 1931 he was adult education lecturer, tutor, and leader-writer on the staff of the *Sydney Morning Herald*, then served in the A.I.F. artillery and as Deputy Assistant Director, Army Education Service, during the war. Afterwards Associate Professor of Australian Literature at the Australian National University. Publications include three books of poetry: *Adagio in Blue* (1938), *Emu Parade* (1941), and *Bayonet and Grass* (1957); *We're Going Through*, radio verse play (1945); *Six Australian Poets*, criticism (1942). He has also edited *Selected Poems of Henry Kendall* (1957), and anthologies.

pp.—33-36

MUDIE, Ian. Born at Hawthorn, South Australia, in 1911, and educated at Scotch College, Adelaide. He has worked as farm-hand, freelance journalist, manager of a real-estate agency, and is now editor of the publishing firm of Rigby's Ltd, Adelaide. Most of the contents of several previous books of verse were collected in *Poems 1934-1944* (1945), and he has since published *The North-bound Rider* (1963).

pp.—83-86

MURPHY, R. D. Born at Cooma, N.S.W., in 1910. He was educated at Marist Brothers' High School, Darlinghurst, became a Marist Brother and has taught English in various schools of the Order in N.S.W., Victoria and S.A. He has published one volume of verse, *Speak to Strangers* (1960).

pp.—77-78

PICOT, James; 1906-1944. Born at Baldock in Hertfordshire, England. He came to Australia in 1923 and worked on farms in the Darling Downs. Graduating in Arts at Brisbane University, he became a Licentiate of Theology (Anglican) but was never ordained. He served in Malaya with the Australian military forces in World War II and died in a prison camp in Siam. *With a Hawk's Quill* was published posthumously in 1953.

p.—50

PORTER, Hal. Born at Albert Park, Melbourne, in 1917, and brought up and educated in Bairnsdale, Gippsland. He became a schoolmaster in Australia and Japan, afterwards a librarian. Since 1961 he has devoted himself to literature. His publications include two novels (*A Handful of Pennies* and *The Tilted Cross*) written under Commonwealth Literary Fund fellowships. Other publications are: *The Hexagon*, poems (1956), *A Bachelor's Children*, short-stories (1962), *The Tower*, play (1963), and *The Watcher on the Cast-iron Balcony* (1963), the first volume of a proposed three-volume autobiography.

pp.—138-139

PORTER, Peter. Born in Brisbane in 1929 and educated at a local public school. He has been amongst other things, a newspaper cadet reporter, wholesale warehouseman, clerk, bookshop assistant, advertising copywriter, and occasionally unemployed, and has written poetry regularly since his 'teens. His poems have appeared in all the major periodicals in England and his first book, *Once Bitten Twice Bitten*, was published in 1961.

pp.—192-193

RIDDELL, Elizabeth (Mrs E. N. Greatorex). Born at Napier, New Zealand, in 1909, and educated at private schools. She came to Australia in 1930 and worked as a journalist on *Smith's Weekly* and the Sydney *Sunday Sun*. After some years overseas as a journalist and war correspondent she returned to Australia and edited a national women's magazine. Publications: *The Untrammelled* (1940), *Poems* (1948), *Forbears* (1961).

pp.—75-77

ROBINSON, Roland Edward. Born at Belbriggan, Ireland, in 1912, and came to Australia at the age of nine. He went to what was then a school in the bush at Blakehurst, N.S.W. At fourteen he was working as a houseboy on the sheep station Caralulup

at Coonamble, N.S.W. He became a shearers' rouseabout, bound-
ary-rider, etc., and a jockey at country "grass-fed" race-meetings.
Through a cleaning job, he became a member and dancer of the
Kirsova Ballet for three years. He has travelled many times to
the Northern Territory and the Centre, gathering aboriginal
mythology. He is a ballet critic and book reviewer for the *Sydney
Morning Herald*, also assistant greenkeeper on Woollahra golf
course. Publications, besides prose works, are: *Beyond the Grass-
tree Spears* (1944), *Language of the Sand* (1949), *Tumult of the
Swans* (1954), *Deep Well* (1962).

pp.—87-89

ROLLS, Eric. Born at Grenfell, N.S.W. in 1923, and educated
at Fort Street High School, Sydney. He served with the A.I.F. in
New Guinea and Bougainville during World War II, and now
owns a farm near Boggabri, N.S.W. His poems, published in
various magazines and anthologies, have not yet been collected
in book form.

pp.—172-174

ROWBOTHAM, David. Born at Toowoomba on the Darling
Downs, Queensland, in 1924, and educated at Toowoomba Gram-
mar School, the State Teachers' College, and Queensland and
Sydney Universities. He served with the R.A.A.F. in the South-
west Pacific, and, after the war, left teaching to enter journalism,
subsequently travelling in Europe. In 1955 he joined the Brisbane
Courier-Mail, where he is literary and theatre critic. He has lec-
tured for the Commonwealth Literary Fund at several Austra-
lian Universities, and has widely toured his own State for the
Fund and Adult Education. His books include *Ploughman and
Poet* (1954), *Inland* (1958), *All the Room* (1963), verse collec-
tions; *Town and City*, stories (1956); and *The Man in the
Jungle*, novel (1964). He is married, and has two daughters.

pp.—174-176

ROWLAND, J. R. Born at Armidale, N.S.W., in 1925, and educated in Sydney. He is a member of the Australian foreign service, and has published verse in various periodicals and anthologies.

pp.—180-182

SHAPCOTT, Thomas William. Born at Ipswich, Queensland, in 1935, the younger of twins. He left school at fifteen after passing his Junior Public Examination from the Ipswich Grammar School. He is a Public Accountant by profession and now lives at Brookfield, Brisbane, sharing 2½ acres with gum-trees, long grass, his neighbour's horses, his wife and two daughters. His first poem was published in the *Bulletin* in 1956 and he has since appeared in all the main Australian literary journals. *Time on Fire* (1961), his first book of verse, was awarded the Grace Leven Prize.

pp.—206-207

SIMPSON, R. A. Born in Melbourne in 1929, and educated at various schools, the Melbourne Teachers' College, and the Royal Melbourne Institute of Technology. Art teacher. During 1957 visited England. Now with the publications branch of the Victorian Education Department. Publications: *The Walk Along the Beach* (1960), *This Real Pompeii* (1963).

p.—194

SLESSOR, Kenneth. Born at Orange, N.S.W., in 1901, and educated at Shore. Reporter Sydney *Sun* 1920-1924; chief sub-editor Melbourne *Punch*, feature writer Melbourne *Herald*, 1925-26; special writer, Sydney *Sun* 1926-27; sub-editor and special writer, *Smith's Weekly* and Sydney *Daily Guardian*, 1927; editor and editor-in-chief, *Smith's Weekly*, 1935-1939; Australian Official War Correspondent (United Kingdom, Greece, Palestine, Syria, Egypt, New Guinea) 1940-1944; leader writer and literary editor, Sydney *Sun*, 1944-1957; leader writer and book reviewer, Sydney *Daily Telegraph* from 1957. Member of the Advisory Board of the Commonwealth Literary Fund from 1953; editor of *Southerly*, 1956-1961; edited (with R. G. Howarth and John Thompson) Penguin book of *Modern Australian Verse*. President of The Journalists' Club, Sydney. O.B.E., 1959. Publications include *Earth Visitors* (1926), *Cuckooz Contrey* (1932), *Five Bells* (1939), *One Hundred Poems* (1944), reprinted 1947, 1951, *Poems* (1957) reprinted in Sirius Books 1962, 1964.

pp.—1-13

SMITH, Vivian. Born at Hobart, Tasmania, in 1933, and educated at the Hobart High School and the University of Tasmania where he is now a lecturer in French. He has published one collection of poems, *The Other Meaning* (1956). One of his poems in the present anthology, "Bedlam Hills", has been set to music by the Australian composer James Penberthy.

pp.—201-202

STEWART, Douglas. Born at Eltham, New Zealand, in 1913, and educated at New Plymouth Boys' High School and Victoria University College. From 1939 to 1961, when he joined the editorial staff of Angus and Robertson, he was editor of the "Red Page" of the *Bulletin*. Married to artist Margaret Coen. He has published, besides short-stories and criticism, the verse plays *Ned Kelly* (1943), *The Fire on the Snow* (1944), *The Golden Lover* (1944), and *Shipwreck* (1947), also a number of books of verse, of which the most recent is *Rutherford* (1963).

pp.—102-109

STEWART, Harold. Born in Sydney in 1916, and educated at Drummoyne Public School, Fort Street High School, the Conservatorium of Music and the University of Sydney. Publications: *Phoenix Wings* (1948), *Orpheus* (1956).

pp.—129-131

STOW, Randolph. Born at Geraldton, W.A., in 1935, and educated locally and at Guildford Grammar School and the Univer-

sity of Western Australia; since graduation has worked on a
mission in N.W. Australia, as a jackaroo anthropologist in New
Guinea, lived in East Anglia, the Highlands of Scotland, and
Malta, and in between times taught English at the Universities
of Adelaide, Leeds and Western Australia. Publications: Novels:
A Haunted Land (1956), *The Bystander* (1957), *To The Islands*
(1958), *Tourmaline* (1963); Verse: *Act One* (1957), *Outrider*
(1962).

pp.—211-215

THIELE, Colin. Born at Eudunda, S.A., in 1920, and educated
at various country high schools. He later became a graduate and
prizeman of Adelaide University, and a Fulbright scholar. After
service in the R.A.A.F. he returned to the S.A. Education De-
partment, and became vice-principal of Wattle Park Teachers'
College, Adelaide. He has done much writing for radio and tele-
vision, including plays such as *Burke and Wills*, *Edward John
Eyre*, and *The Shark Fishers*. His books include *Progress to De-
nial*, which won the Miles Memorial Poetry Prize in 1945, and
Man in a Landscape, which was awarded the Grace Leven Poetry
Prize in 1961. He has also written *The Sun on the Stubble*, a
humorous novel of rural life in a S.A. German farming com-
munity. He is married, with two daughters.

pp.—152-154

THOMPSON, John. Born in Melbourne in 1907, and educated
at Melbourne Grammar and Melbourne University. He lived in
England for several years and joined the A.B.C. in 1939. He
served in the A.I.F., was A.B.C. War Correspondent in Java, and
has since made literary and documentary programmes for the
A.B.C. in Australia and several other countries. Married, with
two sons. Publications: four books of verse, including *I Hate and
I Love* (1963), and two books of prose, *Hubbub in Java* and *On
Lips of Living Men*.

pp.—63-67

THWAITES, Michael. Born in Brisbane in 1915, and educated at Geelong Grammar School and Melbourne University. He was Rhodes Scholar for Victoria in 1937; and while at Oxford won the Newdigate Prize and the King's Medal for Poetry with his long poem "Milton Blind". After serving as commander of a corvette with the R.N.V.R. in World War II, he took his B.Litt. at Oxford, and returned in 1947 to lecture at Melbourne University. He is now a member of the Commonwealth Civil Service. He lives in Melbourne and is married, with four children. Publications: *Milton Blind* (1938), *The Jervis Bay* (1943).

pp.—119-121

VALLIS, Val. Born at Gladstone, Queensland, in 1916, and educated at Rockhampton High School. After serving with the Army in Australia and New Guinea during World War II, he took his B.A. at the University of Queensland in 1950 and subsequently his Ph.D. at the University of London. He is senior lecturer in aesthetics at the University of Queensland. Publications: *Songs of the East Coast* (1948), *Dark Wind Blowing* (1961).

pp.—131-133

VREPONT, Brian (B. A. Truebridge); 1882-1955. Born in Melbourne and became a goldminer in Queensland, masseur, busker, employee in Angus and Robertson's bookshop, Sydney, and a music teacher. Publications: *Plays and Flower Verses for Youth* (1934), *The Miracle* (1939), *Beyond the Claw* (1943).

pp.—20-22

WALLACE-CRABBE, Chris. Born at Melbourne in 1934 and educated at Scotch College and the University of Melbourne. After an assortment of occupations, he became Lockie Fellow in Australian Literature and Creative Writing at the same University. He has published *The Music of Division* (1959) and *In Light and Darkness* (1964), as well as editing *Six Voices*: Contemporary Australian Poets (1963).

pp.—203-205

WEBB, Francis. Born in Adelaide in 1925, and educated at the Christian Brothers schools at Chatswood and Lewisham in Sydney. He served in Canada with the R.A.A.F. in World War II and, after some years spent subsequently in Canada and England, now lives in Australia. Publications: *A Drum for Ben Boyd* (1948), *Leichhardt in Theatre* (1952), *Birthday* (1953), *Socrates* (1961).

pp.—183-189

WOOD, A. J. Born at Lake Cargelligo, N.S.W., in 1906, and educated at Hurlstone Agricultural High School and Sydney and Melbourne Universities. He has been a grazier in Victoria and western New South Wales, and subsequently became interested in rutile mining. His poems have appeared in magazines and anthologies.

pp.—51-52

WRIGHT, Judith (Mrs J. P. McKinney). Born at Thalgarrah near Armidale in N.S.W., and educated by Correspondence School and at New England Girls' School and the University of Sydney. After a year abroad, worked in Sydney at various secretarial jobs, later at the University of Queensland as statistician. Now married, with one daughter, lives at Tamborine in Queensland. Commonwealth Literary Fund Scholarships 1949 and 1962; has lectured for C.L.F. at various Australian universities. Her books of verse are: *The Moving Image* (1946), *Woman to Man* (1949), *The Gateway* (1953), *The Two Fires* (1955), *Birds* (1963), *Five Senses*, selected poems (Sirius Books, 1963). *The Generations of Men* (biography) was published in 1959, and she has also written criticism and children's books.

pp.—121-128

INDEX OF TITLES